Transcribing and Editing Oral History

by Willa K. Baum

American Association for State and Local History

Nashville

Published by the American Association for State and Local History, an international nonprofit membership organization. For membership information, please contact Membership Services, (615) 255-2971.

95 94 93 92 91   9   8   7   6   5

Publication of this book was made possible in part by funds from the sale of the Bicentennial State Histories.

Library of Congress Cataloging-in-Publication Data

Baum, Willa K
    Transcribing and editing oral history.

    Bibliography: p. 123
    1. Oral history. I. Title.
D16.14.B38   907'.2   77-3340
ISBN 0-910050-26-0

Contents

1

Introduction

Oral history is a modern research technique for preserving knowledge of historical events as recounted by participants. It involves the tape recording of an interview with a knowledgeable person, someone who knows whereof he or she speaks from personal participation or observation, about a subject of historical interest. Oral history interviews, as differentiated from specific historical research, are intended for the widest possible use, both present and future. Therefore, the scope of the subjects discussed is usually wider than for specific research. The resulting tapes must then be preserved and processed in such a way as to make them usable, and accessible.

There are four steps to oral history: creating, processing, curating, and finally, using. This guide will deal only with the second step, *processing*—a term which includes both transcribing and editing.

The first step, creating, is focused on collecting material that will be of value and be historically authentic (based on fact) and to that end it involves the careful selection of narrators and well-planned questioning.

Processing focuses on making the material collected as accessible (you can find it and you have permission to use it) and usable (in a form and a degree of understandability to be used fairly easily) as possible. Processing can also provide a second chance to increase historical authenticity if one asks the narrator to review the transcript and calls his/her attention to passages that are unclear or questionable. One must be sensitive to the possible effects of preparing oral history transcripts for publications or public view. Processing done well may present the opportunity to build community iden-

5

tity and to bestow a feeling of recognition and dignity on the older members of the community; done poorly, the remote but persistent danger exists of wreaking social injury on the community.

It is at the processing step that substantial questions arise in oral history circles as to whether the authenticity that is sought is to the facts of the historical events being discussed in the interview, or the facts of what actually took place at the time of the interview itself. And questions arise as to whether, in the interests of accessibility and usability, you can reorder the information given if it is seriously out of place—and therefore hard to find or to follow. You may also wonder if you can alter the wording slightly to make the statements more understandable. How you handle every step of the oral history process, from the interviewing session down to the presentation of the completed manuscript, will depend on whether you put primary emphasis on authenticating the interview session or on the events described in the interview. The question will be discussed further in the chapter on editing.

Step three, curating, deals with the whole problem of preserving the tapes, transcripts, and other supplementary materials: filing them in such a way that they can be found and made available for use without damage to the materials; developing finding aids such as catalog cards, bibliographies, regional and subject listings, and publicity. Step four, using, deals with the suitable and unsuitable uses of oral history materials, how the researcher can find them, and proper ways of quoting them.

There are no cut and dried rules for how to do oral history at any step. Oral history is an art, not an exact science. It is important that each program work out its own goals and methods. These should take into consideration the strengths and weaknesses of the staff as well as the goals and the realities of the program's situation. There are different ways to go about oral history; the results may differ, but each may be equally valuable.

Every step of the way in oral history involves making a decision. Whom to interview? For one session or many? What question to ask next? How to phrase it? Whether to transcribe the interviews or just aim at indexing the tapes? How lightly or heavily to edit the transcripts? How roughly or elegantly to complete the transcript? How fully to index? If you don't like decision-making, avoid oral history.

In this booklet on processing, I have tried to spell out some of the alternatives, and to indicate what my recommendation would be. You must fit this to your own program's situation. Setting up your program's policies should involve a good bit of discussion within the staff, for every staff member ought to understand the why and where-for of each step. There is too much judgment and discrimination involved in oral history work for the staff to be able to function by rote.

I have started with a few premises that I should make clear. First, I have assumed that your oral history program, like most others, is underfunded and understaffed, and that many or all of the staff are volunteers. Second, that the information the program is trying to gather is for a variety of uses, primary of which is community use, and that specific academic research is a secondary use. Third, that your information is primarily about historical events, institutions, places, persons, and ways of life, and only secondarily about how the narrators feel about life or how they relate to the interviewer. This is a crucial premise when one considers how to transcribe and how to edit.

And for purposes of writing style, I have arbitrarily designated all narrators female and all oral history staff male. This is not because women talk better and men process better, but simply because, while all aspects of oral history can be equally well done by males or females, it becomes cumbersone to write about "he/she delivering his/her transcript to him/her." Therefore, for the duration of this book, please accept that she/her relates to narrators and he/him relates to oral history staff and neither has anything to do with gender.

In this book, the word *interview* means one or more recording sessions with one narrator. An interview can represent 15 minutes recording time or it can represent 20 recording sessions, perhaps totalling 30 taped hours and 900 transcript pages.

2

First Steps at the End of the Interview Session

As this book will deal only with processing, we will start as the interviewer turns off the tape recorder following a successful interview. The processing begins in the closing minutes of the interview session.

Interview Notes

During the interview session, the interviewer should keep a running list of names, dates, words or phrases that may be hard to hear, old-fashioned, technical or otherwise difficult for the transcriber. Notes on the subjects discussed are useful for the table of tape contents, or recalling what was covered if there will be another interview session before this one is transcribed. He should also have jottings on the surroundings, appearance of narrator, other persons present, etc.—all to be used in writing up an Interview History—and notes to himself on questions to ask later or facts to look up.

Some projects prepare neat forms for these notes such as a checklist form for names and spelling and a form for description of surroundings. They are a good idea for reminding the interviewer that this information should be collected; but in my experience the interviewer is doing all he can to juggle his question outline, use one notepad for all the above information, keep the tape recorder recording, and still manage a comfortable flow of questions and really listen to what the narrator answers. The neat forms can be filled out later from the rough notes.

At the close of the interview, ask the narrator about the spelling of names or technical words, correct them on your notepad, and mark an OK to show you have checked them (but be aware that the narrator may have the wrong spelling). Do the same for dates.

Fill out the label on the tape box, and also affix a little label with the name of the narrator on the tape reel or cassette. The label should list the following:

Regional Oral History Office
Narrator: *Abe Carlin*
Date: *17 May 1973*   Place: *Oakland, Calif.*
Interviewer: *Mary Fontenrose*
Project Title: *Earl Warren Era Series*
Interview Session: *1*
Length: *1 hour, 15 minutes*

Supporting Papers and Photographs

You will probably want to include with the completed interview one or more photographs of the narrator or events or persons she talks about. You will also want illustrative materials.

If your project is so planned that you interview a great many people briefly, and speed and efficiency is of the essence, then try to collect those items right then. List the items you take, indicate whether you are to keep them or copy and return them, and be sure every photograph is identified in pencil lightly on the back as to names, place, date, event.

Within the next week write a thank-you letter and include a written list of the supporting materials you have taken. Return them later with another letter (even though you do all this by personal delivery). Having such information in writing will avoid later hassles as to whether you did or didn't borrow and return Aunt Minnie's picture.

But if speed is not a prime consideration, and I hope it is not, then it is better not to handle the collecting of supporting materials at the time of the interview. There are too many other details to take care of during the interview. And the interviewer, and especially the narrator, will welcome a later reason to get together again. It is better to just advise the narrator that you will be asking for this sort of material at a later date.

Legal Agreement

It is wise to ask the narrator to sign the legal agreement at the close of the interview session. Most oral history narrators are selected in part for their longevity and they may already be at an age when actuarial statistics are against them. The sooner you take care of that detail, the better.

You can explain that this release will enable you to proceed with the processing; that if you are able to transcribe, you will submit the transcript to them for their review and approval, and that at that time they will have an opportunity to reconsider the agreement and add restrictions if they wish. If they are very apprehensive and will not sign a full release, you can offer to restrict the use of the interview tape for the present, and remove the restrictions after they have approved the transcript. A future date could be designated, in the event the tape is never transcribed or the narrator is not able to review it. I do not recommend working out restrictions at the time of the interview. You will both be tired, and the narrator will be inclined to request more restrictions than she will later on after thinking about what she said or after reviewing the transcript. See Chapter 9, p. 73, for fuller discussion of the legal agreement.

A Table of Tape Contents

On the interviewer's return from the interview and before returning the tape recorder, the most efficient next step is to listen to the entire tape, make a rough table of tape contents, and jot down personal notes as to whether to interview this narrator further and what questions to ask. It is also an opportunity to evaluate one's own interview technique.

At this point you may not know if the tape will be transcribed or not. But whether the project does intend to transcribe this tape, or conversely, intends to deposit the tape as is with only a carefully prepared tape index, it is still worthwhile for the interviewer to make a rough table of contents. The best laid plans often go awry; and the

TABLE OF TAPE CONTENTS

Tape Number___1___

Narrator: _Captain Hans Hanson_____Occupation: _Ship Captain - PACIFIC QUEEN_

Address: ___1742 Filbert Street, San Francisco, California_____

Length: _1 hour_

Date of Interview:___7 September 1974_____Session: ___1___Place: _____Capt. Hanson's
                                                          home, S.F.

Title or Subject: ___Shipwreck of PACIFIC QUEEN, 1938_____

Interviewer: _Mary Fontenrose_____Others Present: _Mrs. Gertrude Hanson, wife of_
                                                         Captain Hanson

CONTENTS:

Min.	Counter	
	25	Childhood in Sweden (near Stockholm).
		Shipping out on German ship, to Mexico. Capt. Kniesche.
	80	Jump ship in Santa Rosalia, Mexico; train to San Francisco.
5	120	Shipping out from San Francisco, 1905–1909. Coastwise lumber ships.
10	250	Move to Australia, 1909–1912.
15	350	World War I, unable to sign up with buddies, all his buddies killed. Stowaway to San Francisco again.
20	488	Citizenship in U.S., 1918; marriage, Ann Walden Hanson, 1919. Studying for second mate's license.
25	610	Working for Swayne & Hoyte Steamship Co., 1920–1938. World War II, supervising shipbuilding in Richmond, California.
30	725	Retirement to Bolinas. Wife's death, 1970; second marriage, 1973, Gertrude Olson Hanson.
35	844	Shipwreck of Pacific Queen, 1938. Failure of dynamo; efforts to turn engine on. Collision with lumbership.
40	876	Seven crew killed—engine room, messroom, steerage. Four passengers killed—mother & children, race horse stableman. Insurance Inquiry.
SIDE 2		Comments on shipping conditions. Wages, pilot responsibilities, conflicts with Sailors Union
5	122	Pilots
10	250	Conflicts with Sailors Union; Andrew Furuseth, Harry Bridges.

Fig. 1. Sample table of tape contents.

transcribing step is the most likely place for oral history projects to falter, get hopelessly backlogged, and even lose heart and fail. With a rough table of contents, the interview is immediately usable. The table of tape contents can be useful in determining whether the tape should be transcribed or not. If you do decide to transcribe, the table of tape contents will serve as a guide to the transcriber and will be an aid to the editor in setting up headings for the transcript. It will always serve as a finding aid to portions of the tape, even if there is a transcript.

The table of tape contents should list in order subjects discussed, localities and dates, names of persons mentioned. It need not be as full as the interview notes, which will be kept with the tape and the table of tape contents.

There is no simple, satisfactory way to indicate the location of a passage on the tape. There are elaborate systems involving four-track or eight-track tapes, with beeps at regular intervals on one track, but these are unrealistic for the modest oral history project. One can use the digital counter on the tape recorder, or time segments. Neither one is very accurate, but each will get you to somewhere in the right vicinity. The more detailed the table of tape contents, the more easily a user can figure out whether to go forward or backward to locate the passages he is interested in.

Fig. 1 is a sample table of tape contents, using both digital counter and time segments.

Preparing an Archival Copy of the Tape

Not all projects will have either the funds or the need to prepare a permanent archival copy of their tapes. But if that is to be done, the time to do it is as soon as the interviewer turns in the tape and before any work begins on the tape.

The best sound is on the original recording tape; any copies will be slightly inferior. Sound is best preserved on 1½ mil polyester, reel-to-reel tape. The thinner the tape, the more possibility that over time there will be a print-through of sound. So the ideal system would be to do the recording on 1½ mil, reel-to-reel tape, preserve that original recording as the archival tape, and make a working library-use copy on either cassette or reel-to-reel.

In fact, with the rapid disappearance of portable reel-to-reel tape recorders, you will probably have to record on cassette, make an archival copy on reel-to-reel, and use the original recording cassette for your working and library-use copy.

Or, even more realistically, you will not be able to afford to make any copies at all and you will just poke out the two little tabs in the back of your cassette so the tape cannot be erased and that original recording will serve all purposes.

3
The Big Decision:
Whether to Transcribe or Not

Whether to transcribe the tape or merely to prepare a tape index and deposit them as tapes is the major decision in the processing of oral history interviews. If you do decide to transcribe, you are committing the project to a number of costly and time-consuming steps. If your project is committed to seeking approval of the narrator, you must then submit the transcript to her for review, with the attendant danger that she may not approve it. If you decide not to transcribe, once the interview is taped, the job is almost completed—and the tapes may never be used. The question comes down essentially to costs vs. usability. It may not be advisable to submit the transcript for approval in some sorts of projects. See the discussion .

Why Transcribe?

1. Transcripts are easier to use than tapes, especially if suitably indexed. In fact, few researchers will spend the time to listen to tapes if they are not transcribed. Therefore, if you have put in the great time and expense necessary to recording a well done oral history project, it is a shame not to put it in a form researchers will use.

2. The narrator can correct and amplify what she said in the interview if there is a transcript. Despite the danger of the narrator's deleting important information, most interviews are substantially improved in detail and accuracy by the narrator's review.

3. Your project will have something to show for your efforts, as will your narrators. A shelf of neatly bound transcripts will be a source of pride to the project and the community. It is hard to work up much enthusiasm or funds on the basis of a stack of tapes (although a multi-media tape-slide show can be an effective product).

My recommendation is that a project plan to transcribe and process as many interviews as possible. Despite all the costs and effort involved, if the oral history project is going to fulfill its aims of providing fresh, detailed, reasonably authentic historical data which will be used by researchers, writers, teachers, and the public, then the interviews almost have to be transcribed. But there needs to be room for flexibility. Guidelines should be established so that, depending on the budget and the work staff available, some tapes can be transcribed in their entirety, some partially, and some not at all.

What Not to Transcribe

1. Interviews for which you have no funds nor volunteer typists. If you can't transcribe, you can't; but don't let that be a reason for not continuing the taping program. Record the interviews, make a skimpy or full index of the tape as your time allows, get a signed release from the narrator, and hope the time will come when you can transcribe at least the best tapes.

2. Interviews on a single topic of very limited research value, perhaps the disputed municipal election of 1964, notorious for the chicanery involved but hardly world shaking in its outcome. By doing the recording, you have done your duty for the few researchers who will ever want to hear it. Index and catalog the tape collection and consider it a job adequately done.

3. Interviews with old-timers for which the greatest use will be in the sound and the feeling, language, and flavor it conveys rather than any new information. This kind of tape can be used in teaching, on the radio, with slides to capture the feeling of an era and to give life to history. This is better done by the tape than by a bloodless transcript. Put your efforts into a comprehensive, full tape index and into

making known the value and richness of your aural resources. In folklore projects, where the focus is on the person, you may wish to transcribe some dialect.

4. Interviews that come out badly for one reason or another. Sometimes you select the wrong narrator. It is wise not to commit yourself definitely to transcribing any or all of the tapes with any narrator until you hear what you've got on the tape.

5. There are many projects involving music history.

What to Transcribe

1. Interviews of wide interest, either with persons or about events that you can anticipate will be the subject of research or writing by users.

2. Interviews in which you have already invested a great deal of research time, and which have turned out well.

3. Interviews the project is committed to processing and the donor wants to see—i.e., honorary autobiographies funded by a group of the narrator's admirers, histories of an institution or company for which the project received a grant, and other interviews that were funded with the expectation there would be a finished transcript.

In other words, work out a set of priorities as to which tapes must be transcribed, which should be done because of their broad value, which can be postponed if necessary because of lower expected usability, and which do not justify full processing in terms of their quality or expected usefulness.

If You Don't Transcribe, Indexing the Tape

An index is even more essential to a tape than to a transcript for users are too impatient to listen to hours of tapes in hopes they will find something about their topic of research. A tape can be indexed by the same methods as a transcript (described later in the Indexing section). Rather, the table of tape contents can be indexed if it is detailed enough to include proper names.

If you decide not to transcribe, then the rough table of tape contents should be rewritten in greater detail. This should be done as soon after the interviewing as possible, and preferably by the inter-

viewer. Once a fully detailed table of tape contents has been prepared, it can be used in the same way as the transcript for preparing
an interview index and cards for inclusion in a cumulative index to
the entire collection. For a tape index, use the digital counter numbers in place of transcript page numbers, or divide the tape into
5-minute sections, nine sections to a 45-minute side.

For example, the tape of the interview with Capt. Hanson, p. 11,
could be indexed thus:

	Tape	Side	Counter Number
coastwise shipping	1/	1/	120–250
Kniesche, Capt.	1/	1/	25 (or section 1—first 5 minutes)
lumber, shipping	1/	1/	120–250
Pacific Queen, shipwreck of	1/	1/	844–900
sailors, conditions of work	1/	2/	0–250
ship pilots	1/	2/	122
Swayne & Hoyt Steamship Co.	1/	1/	610

Some oral history programs have used the tape counter numbers
on the transcript instead of transcript page numbers; thus when they
index, the index lists the tape location which is also the transcript
location. Such a numbering system precludes the possibility of reordering any of the spoken material in the transcript. It is a good
system if you anticipate heavy use of the tapes and no necessity to
improve the organization of the interview by moving any sections
around. Keep in mind that tape recorder counter numbers are only
approximate, and less approximate when you play the tape back on
another recorder, which will almost always be the case once the tapes
are deposited in a library.

4

Steps in Processing

Time Required for Each Step

As an aid to considering what is involved in the decision to transcribe, the steps in processing are listed below with the average time required to carry out each step. These are based on one interview session of about an hour and a half, the average length of time for a session. Of course there is a wide variation in the actual number of hours required to perform each task; interviews differ considerably in their complexity, and workers differ in their experience, skill, and speed in carrying out the tasks. In the example given here, 63 hours were needed to process 1½ hour interview.

One Interview Session (1 to 1½ hours)	Hours
Transcribing the tape [the result is a neat transcript with typing errors corrected, 44 pages, double-spaced]	11
Editing & Chaptering [preparing the transcript for review by auditing and light editing, checking facts and adding questions, putting in chapter headings and subheadings]	10
Final typing [about 40 pages, single-spaced, including introductory material and index]	10
Proofreading & Indexing the final typed transcript	8
Introduction & Supplementary Material [writing an interview history and any other explanatory material, collecting photographs and illustrative materials, and writing captions or descriptions of papers]	7
Final Preparation [all of the clerical details required to end up with a finished transcript, as copying photographs, typing captions, manuscript corrections, xeroxing, assembly of transcript, binding]	9

Arrangements [this term covers all the dealings with the narrator
following the interviewing, and can vary from two hours to infinity.
It includes all visits, letters, and telephone calls to the narrator;
delivery and retrieval of the transcript; going over any questions,
corrections, additions, or deletions; legal agreements; and letters of
thanks]   8

The project can decide to cut some of these tasks. For example,
the corrected transcript can be deposited just as it is returned by the
narrator and without all the final work. It can even be submitted to
the narrator with almost no editing, and without chaptering. Elimi-
nation of these steps will save much time which can be invested
instead in more interviews. It may also reduce the satisfaction of
staff, narrators, the community, and users in the product.

The step that cannot be eliminated is "Arrangements," a step our
staff calls "hand-holding" when it exceeds the eight-hour average.

Keeping Track

It is important to have a way to keep track of the progress of each
interview through the many steps in its production. In a small project
with very few workers, record keeping should be minimal, but as the
project expands, it will be necessary to increase the paper work.

The following Interview Production Sheet can be adapted to fit
the steps the project decides on. Use the names, not the initials, for
workers; it is hard enough to decipher the hurriedly scribbled initials
of present staff members, but when the Interview Production Sheets
relate to interviews five or more years old, it becomes impossible (and
it will take five or more years to complete some of your interviews.)

In a small project, each worker can be responsible for filling in
the Interview Production Sheet when he begins or completes a task.

In addition, we find it useful in our office to keep a log, a
chronological notebook in which each worker notes down, for example, when he takes an assignment, when it is finished and how many
hours it took, the taping of an interview, the receipt of a corrected
transcript from a narrator, the receipt of a signed legal agreement.
From the log, the project director can see at a glance what each person
is working on and what his rate of production is.

INTERVIEW PRODUCTION SHEET

SERIES _San Francisco Bay Maritime Series_   NARRATOR _Capt. Hans Hanson_

INTERVIEWER _Mary Fontenrose_

Fill in your name and date of work assigned, received, or completed by you; all transactions re

INVITATION LETTER: Date Sent _18 July 1974_   Date Returned _30 July 1974_

TRANSCRIBING NOT DONE: Reason _____ Tape Index Completed _____ Time_____

TRANSCRIBING:	Interview Date	Transcriber	Date Rec'd by Trnscrb.	Date Compl by Trnscrb.	Pages	Time
#1	9/7/74	Lee Steinback	10/5/74	10/10/74	40	12½ hrs.
#2	9/20/74	Lee Steinback	10/5/74	10/12/74	37	10 hrs
#3						
#4						

EDITING: Editor Name _M. Fontenrose_   Date Rec'd _10/12/74_   Date Compl _11/9/74_ Time _19 hrs_
Edited Copy to Xerox: Date sent _11/12/74_   Date returned _11/13/74_
Edited Copy to Narrator: Date sent _11/25/74_ Date Returned _5/7/75_ Reminder Sent _ _3/3/75_
FINAL TYPING: Typist Name _Keiko Sugimoto_ Date Rec'd _5/15/75_ Date Compl _6/4/75_ Time _21 hrs_

PROOFREADING: Name _M. Fontenrose_   Date Rec'd _6/5/75_   Date Compl _6/15/75_ Time _4 hrs_
INDEXING: Name _M. Fontenrose_   Date Rec'd _6/5/75_   Date Compl _6/15/75_ Time _9 hrs_

FINAL CORRECTIONS: Name _Keiko Sugimoto_ Date Rec'd _6/19/75_ Date Compl _6/24/75_ Time _4 hrs_

INTERVIEW HISTORY: Name _Mary Fontenrose_   Date Compl _6/15/75_

INTRODUCTION: Name _NONE_ Title _____ Date Compl_____

PHOTOS & SUPPORTING DOCUMENTS COMPILED: _3 photographs, newspaper clippings, copy of mate's license._
Photolab—6/17/75

DUPLICATING: Date Sent _7/7/75_ Date Rtrnd _7/12/75_ BINDING: Date Sent _8/6/75_ Date Rtrnd _8/30/75_

LEGAL: Form _A/no restrictions_   Title _Shipwreck of the Pacific Queen, 1938_
To Narrator: Date Sent _9/20/74_ Date Rtrnd _9/20/74_ Executed copy to Narrator _9/20/74_
To Librarian: Date Sent _9/20/74_ Date Rtrnd _9/30/74_ Library copy filed _9/30/74_

DEPOSIT: Bound mss. sent to Narrator _9/12/75_   Bound mss. deposited _10/10/75_
Documents & Photographs Returned to Narrator _6/20/75_   Papers Deposited _10/10/75_
Letter of Thanks sent _9/12/75_   Tapes Deposited _10/10/75_

SPECIAL NOTES: _San Francisco Maritime Museum notified of Capt. Hanson's scrapbooks and ship photographs._
Capt. Hanson's papers donated to San Francisco Maritime Museum, October 1975.
Copy of interview prepared for S.F. Maritime
Museum. Cost $25 paid by Capt. Hanson.   TOTAL COST _$300_

Fig. 2. Sample interview production sheet.

The project director will also need to keep a running list of all interviews in progress and at regular intervals review them to see that all are moving ahead, or if stalled, what can be done to get them moving again. And he will need a list of all workers and what each person's assignments are, so as to know who can take on a new assignment and who are already up to their maximum.

5

Transcribing Procedures

Transcribing Equipment

One can transcribe from any tape recorder simply by hand operating the forward, stop, and reverse buttons. This is slow, and hard on the tape recorder.

If possible, the project should purchase a transcribing machine. A suitable machine will soon pay for itself by the saving in transcribing time. A transcribing machine has foot control for forward, stop, and reverse. Some machines also have a variable speed control allowing the transcriber to slow down the tape as much as 20% and this is a help. In addition to the cost of a transcribing machine, the project should anticipate substantial repair costs—a sad but true fact. The prices and models listed below are subject to change.

Reel-to-Reel Transcribing Machines

> *Tandberg Model 1521F,* $600 complete with footpedal and earphones. A dependable machine used by most oral history offices, 7-inch reels, 3 speeds.

> *Uher 5000,* about $600 complete with footpedal and earphones. Takes 5-inch reels only, 4 speeds.

Cassette Transcribing Machines

> *Craig 2706A,* $250 complete with footpedal and earphones. Variable speed control. This machine can also be used for dictating.

> *Sony BM34,* $500 complete with footpedal and earphones. Vari-

able speed control. This is a heavy-duty machine and is recommended above the light-duty Sony BM25A, $450.

Wollensak 2540AV, $300, plus headphones A-0483, $13, and footpedal A-0542, $47; or $360 complete. Heavy duty, and suitable for recording also, except that its 18 lbs. makes it heavy to carry. It does not have variable speed control.

Dictaphone Model 250, Thoughtmaster, $420 complete with footpedal and earphones. The addition of a dictating microphone at $60 will make this an excellent dictating or recording machine with sound pickup suitable for group interviews. Only 7 lbs. A carrying case is available but at $60 you may prefer to fit out your own case.

Headphones

A better headphone than comes with the transcribing machine may prove of higher acoustical performance and more comfortable to wear as they come with foam ear cushions. Most good headphones are stereophonic. It is therefore necessary to have the seller convert them to monophonic by changing the plug. Select a suitable plug to fit your transcribing machine.

A recommended headphone is Beyer DT302, $24. (Must be converted from stereo to mono)

Tapes

Reel-to-reel. Use 5-inch or 7-inch polyester, 1 mil or 1½ mil thickness. It is not necessary to use the highest fidelity tape (necessary for music only.) Tape of 1½ mil is better for preservation; 1 mil provides longer playing time.

Cassette. Use C-60, middle price quality. C-60 will get 30 minutes on a side, a total of 60 minutes. If you plan to transfer the sound to a 1½ mil reel-to-reel for permanent preservation, go ahead and use C-90 cassettes (45 minutes to a side) which can be used for transcribing and later research use, but which are too thin for permanent preservation. Never use C-120s, they will break or tangle.

Bolted cases are better than fused; when the tape tangles you can open the case and try to repair it. End alarm is useful if your tape recorder has it.

Microphone

Sony ECM-16, $40. Tie clasp-lapel condensor mic.

We highly recommend this small mic which improves the sound greatly. One is enough, for the narrator. The interviewer can speak up so it will pick up the questions. Well worth the extra cost in reducing transcribing time. Try it with your tape recorder before buying.

Maintenance of Machines and Tapes in the Office

Reel-to-reel. Every month clean the heads with Q-tips and head cleaner (about 79¢ a bottle). Demagnetize the head about every 60–70 hours. A head demagnetizer costs about $5.

Cassette. Run a Cassette Head Cleaner tape ($2) through about every month. Run a Demagnetizer Head Cleaner Tape ($6) through about every three months. Run it through forward; *don't rewind* until much later after the tape has demagnetized itself or you just put the charge back on.

Tapes. Store and work with tapes in a room as near to clean room conditions as possible; that is, no smoking, drinking, or eating within 10 feet of tape area. Keep room vacuumed and dusted.

Humidity should be between 40% to 60%, temperature 65°F to 80°F. (These are good conditions for humans as well as tapes.) Do not leave tapes in direct sunlight or near a heater. Put the tape away in its box when it is not being worked with. Handle the tape reel by the hub so as not to damage the flanges. If the reel is damaged, rewind tape to a new reel and throw the damaged reel away. Store tapes in their box, on edge.

Who Should Transcribe

Transcribing is a demanding and rewarding task that requires far more than typing skill. Next to the interviewer, the transcriber is the person who learns the most from the interview. In selecting transcribers, look for the following qualities.

1. Good typing skills, with accuracy more important than speed.

2. The ability to hear electronic sound. Try prospective transcribers out on some tapes; not everyone has a good ear for electronic sound.

3. As broad a general background as possible. The more the transcriber knows about the topic under discussion, the better he will be able to hear and spell it. There is a problem of generation gap between older narrators and young typists, some of whom have never heard the names and phrases the narrator is using and therefore cannot decipher them from the tape.

4. A good knowledge of spelling and punctuation and how to use punctuation to indicate meaning.

5. Having selected some competent transcribers, try to assign the same transcriber for all the tapes with one narrator. And try to assign the same transcriber to all the interviews on one or related subjects.

6. The best person to do the transcribing and the editing is the interviewer. If it is possible to have one person carry out the entire interview (with the exception, perhaps, of the final typing), it will be a better product.

7. Free labor. If you are offered the services of an advanced high school or business college typing class, forget all of the above qualifications and accept. You may have to listen carefully to all the tapes and check them against the transcripts (audit the tapes) and you may even have to retype the corrected transcripts before presenting them to the narrators, but if the typists are any good at all, you will save typing time and your project will be providing invaluable training for prospective job-seekers.

Considerations to Keep in Mind

Transcribing is a work of art, a little akin to translating from one language to another, but with less latitude allowable. The spoken word has many dimensions with which to convey fact and feeling: pitch, loudness, strength, speed, pronunciation, sounds that are not words. In putting a spoken performance down on paper, the transcriber has only words and punctuation to work with. With these, he must try to be accurate as to the information that was related, to use the words that the narrator used, and to catch as closely as possible the flavor and feeling of the speaker. Spoken communication often comes in little bursts of phrases, in incomplete sentences. If put down exactly, they may make the speaker appear to be less literate or well-spoken than in fact she is. And the user may find the transcript hard to follow.

To the delicate task of accurately translating spoken into written language, most oral history projects must add the consideration that the final transcript must be reviewed and approved by the narrator (and each narrator is a different individual with different standards of acceptability.) Projects also will differ in their emphases; some will be primarily seeking to preserve exact information about past events; others will be after attitudes and feelings; still others may be looking for specialized speech patterns or folk phrases. In each case, there may be different standards as to how absolutely verbatim the interview must be transcribed, as weighed against acceptability by the narrator and usability by researchers.

Whatever the priorities of the project, one modification that is not acceptable is to "improve" on the choice of words or the word order of the narrator. There may be a better word to express the concept (and if the editor is pretty sure the narrator has just used the wrong word, it can be called to the narrator's attention at the time of the review) or the word order may be curious, perhaps because the narrator is foreign-born, but that is the essence of the narrator's individuality and it should not be tampered with. That includes bad grammar and expletives. If the narrator wants to, she can revise or delete during the review.

It should be apparent that, with all these considerations to balance, oral history transcribing is hard work, and few persons can do it more than four hours a day. It is also challenging, instructive, and entertaining.

The suggestions that follow will help in producing a neat transcript that will not have to be retyped before presenting it to the narrator for review. The suggestions also presuppose transcribers with a degree of independent judgment.

The Form for Transcripts

1. Make an original and at least one copy. You may prefer to xerox the number of copies you need.

2. Double-space or triple-space. Leave plenty of margin space on sides and bottom. This is to allow for editing, additions, headings, etc.

3. Include the following information at the top of the page, and of all subsequent interviews with the same person:

> *Interview with Bernice H. May, Interview 1*
> *Date of Interview: 15 June 1974; Berkeley, California*
> *Interviewer: Gabrielle Morris*
> *Transcriber: Marilyn White*
> *Begin Tape 1, Side 1*

4. Number the pages consecutively through all the interviews with that narrator; do *not* begin with page 1 again on the second interview.

5. Use last names of speakers if of reasonable length. If not, use initials or an *acceptable* abbreviation. Avoid using two sets of initials as then the reader will have to go through some mental gymnastics each time to figure out who is who. Do not use such non-information designations as Question—Answer or Interviewer—Smith. Examples:

> *Teiser:*
> *Kennedy:*
>
> *Teiser:*
> *L. Kennedy* [If the interview
> includes another
> *A. Kennedy:* member of the family.]

WCL:	[Walter Clay Lowdermilk —too long a name.]
Chall:	[Interviewer]
Mrs. L:	[Mrs. Lowdermilk—using her initials would make it hard to remember who is who.]

6. Note changes in tape as *End Side 1, Begin Side 2./ End Tape 1./ Begin Tape 2, Side 1./ End of Interview.*

7. Set the digital counter at zero when starting the tape. You will then be able to indicate by counter number the portions that you cannot hear so someone else can try them.

8. If the conversation is carried over to the next page, indicate again at the top of the next page who the speaker is. It should not be necessary on any page to turn back to the previous page to find out who is speaking.

Advice to the Transcriber

1. Listen to about 10 minutes before starting to type in order to catch the manner of speaking, special pronunciations, crutch words, etc. Listen ahead at least a phrase before typing. If the narrator is prone to many false starts, you will have to listen ahead more. If the narrator is fairly deliberate, you can type almost as the words are spoken.

2. Type the words you hear, in the order they are spoken. Listen and type with understanding of what the speaker means, but be careful not to get rolling with the speaker so well that you are inadvertently putting words and phrases into her mouth. Even if the speaker may be awkward, forgetful, or nonverbal, resist the temptation to help out with your own superior vocabulary.

3. Type neatly. While this means typing more slowly and taking the time to make neat corrections, a nice-looking transcript will be more acceptable to the narrator. A narrator is less tempted to revise a neat transcript than one that has many errors xxx'd out.

4. Punctuate according to the sense of the words as spoken. Follow your project's style sheet. Do not be too distressed if your

punctuation does not exactly follow the grammar book punctuation rules. They were devised for writing, and the writer had the option of changing the word order. A transcriber has to do the best he can to indicate how the words were spoken. No changing of word order is allowed.

5. Listen for the end of a sentence; even if it isn't a complete sentence, stop, and start a new sentence. Many narrators go on and on, using an "and" instead of a period. End those run-on sentences at reasonable points, but do not break down a complex clause-speaker into a short sentence John Steinbeck-type speaker.

6. Paragraph when the subject changes. You can often hear a new paragraph in the way a narrator speaks, but even if you can't, watch for subject changes, and start a new paragraph when possible. A long, unbroken monologue is very hard to read.

7. Unusual pronunciation and dropped word endings should not be indicated by phonetic spelling. It is almost impossible to convey pronunciation phonetically, and narrators are offended by a sprinkling of "yeahs," "yups," and "goin's," throughout their transcript even if they said it that way. In writing it looks a lot more folksy than it may have really sounded. Save the tape to indicate pronunciation. However, especially in folklore projects, you may decide to try to transcribe phonetically in order to preserve the dialect.

8. Contractions should be typed as spoken. *I'll look that up; I'm not sure what year it was* offends no one and is more natural than "I will look that up; I am not sure what year it was."

9. Crutch words. Almost everyone speaks with a plentitude of crutch words and gurgles such as "ah," "well," "and then," "of course," "you know," "understand?" "right?" which serve the purpose of either a pause to think of the next thing to say, or a check as to whether the other person is listening. In speaking, crutch words may slip by almost unnoticed, but written down they will leap out from the page as a proclamation that the narrator could not get her thoughts together instantaneously. It is unlikely a narrator will approve and release a transcript full of crutch words; even if she does they will serve to impede the reader and to make the narrator look inadequate. Leave out most crutch words in transcribing if it is apparent that they are just pauses for thought. Leave in a few to show the narrator uses

them, that this is an informal conversation. Leave them in if they have meaning.

10. Interviewer's approval words. Do not transcribe comments of the interviewer which are clearly only to indicate he is listening, such as "my, my," "how interesting," "really?" Like crutch words, they only serve to impede the reader and make the interviewer look like a scatterbrain.

11. Do not transcribe false starts or unfinished sentences if the interviewee clearly reconsiders, stops, and then states it otherwise. Do transcribe if it is information she does not repeat in the revised sentence. In other words, get down all the information, but if she fumbles and then starts again, leave out the fumble.

12. Portions you cannot hear. Listen again. Ask someone else in the office to listen. Don't waste too much time trying to hear what you can't. If you still can't make it out, leave a blank about as long as you think the phrase is (don't underscore) and pencil in lightly the counter number. (Remember, you set the digital counter at zero when you began the tape). The interviewer or editor may be able to hear it later.

13. Portions to be left out. The interviewer may indicate on the interview notes that certain portions are not to be typed, perhaps chit-chat, an irrelevant story, or a repetition of an already told tale. If one aims for an informal interview, it is better to leave the tape running during the interview and then not transcribe irrelevant portions than to call attention to the recorder by turning the tape on and off. Omissions may or may not be indicated, according to the interviewer's request. For example (Interruption by take-off of an airplane, conversation about the hazards of living near an airport) may be fine, but omit (Fourth telling of how she walked ten miles to school and never missed a day.)

14. Stage directions, descriptions of what is happening, or how words are spoken. Use these with discretion and put them in parenthesis. Some are necessary to understand the action, such as *(reading from newspaper), (goes to bookcase to get scrapbook), (Mrs. Packard brings in cookies and tea), (interruption for telephone call), (pause while fire engines go by).*

Others are interpretations of the sound and must be used with care

Interview with Abe Carlin, Interview 1   Earl Warren Series
Date of Interview: 17 May 1973; Oakland, California
Interviewer: Mary Fontenrose
Transcriber: Marie Fernandez
Begin Tape 1, Side 1

MF: I'd like to ask you where you were born and where you

grew up.   **crutch word**

Carlin: Well, I was born in ~~Bare Butt~~ *Bear Butte*, Colorado, ~~of course~~, 1907. **run-on sentence**

~~and~~ *A* as a young boy in 1912, ~~of course,~~ we came to

Oakland. Then I went to school in Oakland—started

going to school as a kid. When my sister started getting a **word**

primer ~~quiver~~ and going off to school, I had to get a *primer* ~~quiver~~ too. **heard wrong**

MF: Where had your parents come from?

Carlin: Well, my father was born in England, of course, and my

mother was born in Canada, ~~of course, and~~ *M* my father

was an immigrant from England over to Canada and he

was in the Northwest Mounted Police for a short while, ~~of~~

~~course, and~~ *T* then he met my mother, I guess, and then

that was that.

~~MF: Oh really.~~ **Omit interviewer's approval words**

Fig. 3. An example of a verbatim transcript illustrating the correct format, and showing words the transcriber could have omitted and words heard wrong or not heard. This corrected transcript has been audited (listened to) but not yet edited.

Carlin: ~~Yeah,~~ *Then* He migrated from the midwest of Canada out to
Bear Butte ~~Bare Butt.~~ That's just between the ~~planes~~ *plains* and the ~~roc-~~
~~kets.~~ *Rockies)*

~~MF: My goodness.~~

false start

Carlin: ~~Yeah.~~ Well, ~~he worked   mined~~ —then he worked for the
mines out there, up in the timber country, ~~and~~ then in
1912 he came down to Oakland, ~~of course,~~ and went to
work on the waterfront there, in Oakland, ~~and~~ then my
mother and the seven kids came out, ~~of course,~~ and
lived in Oakland.

MF: You had six brothers and sisters?

Carlin: Yeah. Four brothers and two sisters. (Gets photo album,
shows pictures.)

MF: My goodness, that's a big family.

Carlin: ~~Yup~~ *Yes* it is. They're all still alive too.

MF: ~~Really?~~ That's a very good record.

~~Carlin: Yeah.~~

MF: What kind of work did your father do on the waterfront?

Fig. 3 (Continued).

Carlin: He was a *wharfinger* — **couldn't hear** there at Central Terminal
and I forget just what year he left there and went to work
for Standard Oil and then, ~~of course~~, he worked for
Standard and from there he retired, ~~and~~ that's many,
many years ago. The dates kind of slip by, you know.

MF: How far did you get in school?

Carlin: Oh, about the seventh grade. I found out that I knew
more than the teachers did, so there wasn't any use in
staying.

MF: Did you ever want to go to college?   **heard**
                it never occurred to me —   **wrong**
Carlin: No, ~~never could be~~.

MF: So then, did you go straight to sea after you left school?

Carlin: No, I worked on the waterfront for a while and then I
grabbed a ship and sailed for a while ~~and~~ then
shipping was very bad, ~~of course~~, and I   **couldn't**
went on the coastal and geodetic survey for about three   **hear**
                        deep - water
years. Then I was back on the ~~damper~~ ships again. I was
sailing there when the '34 strike came on.

Fig. 3 (Continued).

lest they offend the narrator. For example, *(laughter)* is fine if it follows a genuine joke, but may be offensive if it is in an inappropriate place or in fact represents a nervous giggle. The transcriber can try to indicate how the words were spoken—*(softly)*, *(sadly)*, *(whispering)*—and can underline words to indicate heavy emphasis, but keep in mind the narrator's feelings. Some indications of emotions are best limited to the tape where they can be evaluated in their full sound context.

15. Proper names and places. Use the notes that come with the interview. The interviewer should have written down names and places, and checked the spelling with the narrator. If not in the notes, look up any names you can in such reference works as the telephone directory, who's who, almanac, atlas, and history books. If nowhere to be found, spell phonetically. The names that cannot be checked should be called to the attention of the narrator when she reviews the transcript.

Filing the Transcript

File the second copy of the transcript in an "original transcripts" file. This copy is the guide to the tape. It can be modified by auditing (listening to the tape) to correct transcribing errors, but it should not be edited—especially if editing involves moving portions of the transcript around.

However, if the narrator asks that substantive information be deleted (that is, information and not just style changes), then that information must be cut out of the original transcript and destroyed. The portions of the tape on which that information was recorded should be erased. The original transcript can read "Five minutes erased at request of Narrator."

The ribbon copy can be filed in the "To be Edited" file. The tape and any interview notes should be kept with this copy of the transcript as they will be necessary at the next step, auditing or a combined editing-auditing step.

The transcriber should explain any problems he/she encountered in the transcribing to the interviewer. Of course, if the same person is the interviewer, transcriber, and editor, all of these steps can move ahead more efficiently.

Fill in on the Interview Progress Sheet the date of completion, how many hours the transcribing took, and your name.

6

Auditing the Tapes

Auditing combines the concept of hearing with that of verifying the record. In oral history parlance, auditing means listening to the tape and checking it against the transcript to make sure the transcriber heard and typed all the words correctly, did not add any words that were not on the tape, spelled the words correctly, and did a reasonable job of punctuation in order to catch the meaning and emphases of the narrator. It takes at least two hours per one hour of recording to audit adequately.

A Separate Step or Part of Editing

Most proper oral history projects include auditing as an essential step following transcription and preceding editing. A special person is assigned this task, or all of the clerical personnel do a certain amount of it as a break from their other duties.

Because auditing does take a lot of time, I do not consider it essential as a separate step. Instead, the person who will edit the transcript should do so with the tape at hand so that the editing and auditing steps are in fact combined.

However, there are times when separate auditing is essential:

1. When the transcriber is inexperienced (and if you can inveigle the services of an advanced typing class, by all means do so, and by all means, audit.)

2. When the acoustics were especially bad and the transcriber has expressed insecurity about what he put on paper or has had to leave blank.

3. When the transcript is not going to be returned to the narrator and the audited transcript will be the final form of the interview for deposit. If you will not have the advantage of the narrator giving it a last review, then a very careful audit is called for.

Even if not essential, auditing is a useful step if staff time permits, and it can be made multipurpose. For example, auditing can serve as the first training step for new interviewers, and it can serve as a means for other interviewers to become familiar with the information their colleagues are turning up so they can use that background in their own interviews.

How to Audit

1. Listen carefully. A fresh pair of ears may hear things differently. If a word or phrase sounds different than it reads, write it in in pencil above the original. Cross out the original if you are sure; mark it for special attention by the narrator if you are not sure.

2. Consider whether the transcriber has punctuated according to the sense and sound of the narration. The proper punctuation for the spoken word is pretty variable. Use the project's own style guide, and try to be consistent within at least that interview.

3. Consider whether the transcriber has left in too many meaningless gurgles and false starts (cross them out if you feel sure) or has left out a significant gurgle or beginning statement. In case of disagreements, the interviewer should be the arbiter in the office (because the interviewer is the person who had the closest contact with the narrator,) and the narrator should be the final arbiter as to what she really meant to say.

Examples of Mistranscription

The following are some examples of mistranscriptions. Note that in each case the transcriber has tried to understand and make a reasonable statement out of the sounds. The resulting error makes good enough sense that it might well not be caught by either an auditor or an editor who is not familiar with what the narrator would be trying to say. This is another reason for having the editing, and if possible, the transcribing, done by the interviewer.

Some examples of transcribing errors:

Transcription: They had *Larry Baceretti* right under the shadow of Harvard.
Correct: They had *Mary Baker Eddy* right under the shadow of Harvard.
Transcription: Who the hell is *fooling around* with all this? *Who* can't live a separate life?
Correct? Who the hell is *fooling whom* with all this? *You* can't live a separate life.
Transcription: I showed him the budget *which was part of the economy.*
Correct: I showed him the budget *for the Department of Agronomy.*
Transcription: They used to have the *customers* sitting up with the dead.
Correct: They used to have the *custom of* sitting up with the dead.
Transcription: I joined the Elks Club *of Tacoma* over fifty years ago.
Correct: I joined the Elks Club *a little* over fifty years ago.
Transcription: So the city had *a place,* and we had *other places.*
Correct: So the city had *an appraiser* and we had *an appraiser.*
Transcription: *They wouldn't send any money. Unless you ask the brother. . .*
Correct: *Who asks anybody? The less you ask, the better.*
Transcription: He was a *character, for sure.*
Correction: He was a *caricature.*
Transcription: I was appointed to the Task Force on *Economic Gross Inopportunity.*
Correction: I was appointed to the Task Force on *Economic Growth and Opportunity.*
Transcription: That was the first *raise in the marketing* agreement that went into effect.
Correction: That was the first *raisin marketing* agreement that went into effect.

7

Editing

It is a rare conversation that is worth preserving without some editing. But, within limits, one can elect to edit either before the words are spoken or after the interview is in transcript form. By strict adherence to a topical outline of questions, by reinforcement of the narrator's awareness that she is "on the air," and by turning off the recorder when the conversation wanders from the outline, it is possible to produce a well spoken and well organized transcript that will require little editing. This kind of prerecording editing will save many headaches in dealing with the transcript. It may also result in a more stilted manner of speaking and the loss of some of the charm and perhaps important by-ways that a less formal interview would capture. That decision will have been made back at the interviewing step.

Now you have the transcript; it is in good or poor order. What should you do with it next?

There is much disagreement in oral history circles on what should and should not be done in the way of editing. At one extreme are those who argue that the tape recording itself is the primary record and that the transcript must mirror that recording as closely as possible, i.e., an absolutely verbatim transcript with no editing except to correct punctuation and spelling and perhaps add such information as first names and exact dates, carefully bracketed to indicate it was the editor who inserted that. Their goal is to authenticate the interview situation itself, how the narrator and interviewer interacted, what the narrator's state of health and memory was that day, whether the narrator was nervous or comfortable with certain topics, with what degree of feeling the narrator told her tale.

There are others who, in the search for historical authenticity, will argue that the transcript is the beginning framework, but that the editor must work with the narrator in checking facts, correcting unclear statements, and adding details so that the final manuscript is the most accurate account of the events being discussed that that narrator can produce.

Still other oral history programs may not care much at all about what actually happened; what they want is the cultural milieu, the accurate speech patterns, modes of expression, folklore, and feelings of a certain group of persons.

And at the other extreme is the group who will favor rewriting the transcript in perfect English, deleting anything unpleasant about anyone, eliminating interviewer questions, and producing a glowing autobiography in the style of a high school graduation speech. (The latter is often the expectation of the narrator or her family and it may take quite a bit of skilled "handholding" to end up with a more realistic approximation of the interview and the historical truth.)

Each of these methods, and all degrees in between, can be reasonable editing procedures for some oral history programs, depending upon the goals of the program; the last one, though, gets very close to vanity biography and far from oral history. It is evident each program will have to make its own evaluation of what sort of processing to do, especially at the editing step, but also at the transcribing step, and very much at the interviewing step. My own experiences and biases are in the direction of making historical authenticity the prime goal, and the reader should bear that in mind in weighing the suggestions that follow. That may not be your prime goal.

As to the controversy between either documenting the interview itself by means of a verbatim transcript or documenting the events discussed by means of an edited transcript, the problem is easily solved; document it both ways. The tape and the notes taken at the time of the interview together comprise the closest record one can get, short of video taping, of the original interview. Preserve these (if you have the narrator's permission to do so) for research into the interview situation, the narrator's personality, or the verbal culturisms of the narrator and her group.

Then move on to editing the transcript with the goal of producing a manuscript that is the closest possible rendition of the spoken interview and at the same time usable by researchers, historically authentic, and acceptable to the narrator.

Because the goals and situation of oral history projects differ so, I would like to propose several principles to keep in mind rather than a set formula on how one should or should not edit. Each program staff will have to use its own judgment. I do strongly recommend that you aim at doing the least amount of revision you can get away with, within the parameters of the following principles, in order to preserve the flavor of the interview and to lessen the editing time.

General Principles

1. Meet the purposes of your program. Are you mainly trying to get a feel for this narrator, or a clear, accurate account of something that happened? For example, in an interview with a 104-year-old narrator, we did not edit out any ramblings or repetitions because the memory processes of a person of that age were in themselves of interest. For a poet, her stream-of-consciousness account was relevant to how she did her work. For the executive secretary going through a step-by-step account of the growth of a company, it was decided to rearrange the events chronologically; they were scattered because of the long time that had elapsed between interview sessions.

2. Produce as accurate and complete information as possible. This may require editorially adding further information as names and dates, asking the narrator to explain, clarify, or amplify some statements, calling the narrator's attention to statements that seem to be in error.

3. Produce a usable research manuscript. This will involve cutting out unnecessary impediments to the flow of the story, possibly reordering the material so that the researcher can follow it, adding such guides as table of contents, topic headings, and an index.

4. Produce an accurate portrait of the narrator. This means keeping as close to the manner of speaking and order of thought of the narrator as you can. But because oral history programs often record the oldest members of the community, they must deal with the fact

that impairments of age may blur the picture of their narrators. If the portrait sought is of the narrator at her peak, sometimes this will require considerable editorial help in filling in forgotten names, cutting out stammerings and repetitions, and revising nonsequiters based on faulty hearing. (On the other hand, if your purpose is a study of the effects of aging or pain-killing drugs, then a different standard should be used.)

5. Keep one's word with the narrator. In the introductory letter and meeting, or by your behavior, did you indicate that this interview, as spoken, was to be the final version or that it was just a first draft? For example, in the interview session, did you make a formal beginning such as, "This is November 8, 1976, and we are in the home of Senator James F. Smith at 2122 A Street, Central City. Senator Smith has been asked to record for posterity and Central City University the story of his six years in Washington." With an introduction like that, Senator Smith has been alerted to record only what he expects to appear in the final transcript. The more so if the interviewer switches off the recorder when they chit-chat, and announces on the tape after he has turned it over, "Side 2 of an interview with Senator Smith recorded on November 8, 1976." On the other hand, if the interviewer simply switches on the recorder while the preliminary pleasantries are being exchanged, and leaves it on during coffee, he has implicitly indicated there will be a chance to edit. Whatever your agreement with the narrator, explicit or implicit, keep it.

6. If your program has such a provision, produce a manuscript that will be acceptable to the narrator. Unless the narrator approves the manuscript and allows you to deposit it for preservation and use, there is no value at all to all the steps you have taken up to this time, except perhaps your own edification and entertainment. Preparing the transcript for the narrator's approval will involve different degrees of editing, depending on the narrator, and it will require great sensitivity on the part of the editor to gauge what will be acceptable.

7. Avoid personal or social injury to the narrator, persons she discusses, the community, or your own program. This will involve a prudent review of the transcript and consideration of what is historically necessary or not necessary, what might be better made anonymous, what should be closed for a certain time.

Advice to the Editor

In my advice to the editor, I will start with the simplest editing, the sort that is required in every transcript, and then go on to more difficult, and fortunately, less common problems.

The First Reading and Audit Check

[Reread the steps described in the sections on transcribing and auditing; if they have not been taken care of already, this is the time to do so.]

1. Work on a carbon copy of the transcript unless you plan to xerox your edited copy, in which case you can work on the ribbon copy. You should end up with one neatly edited copy to send to the narrator for her review, plus one "insurance copy" of the edited transcript to hold in the office in case the narrator loses or does not return the edited transcript. Remember you have already filed away one verbatim copy of the transcript, to serve as a guide to the tape— no editing on this verbatim copy except corrections of transcribing errors. [You may elect to send the narrator a xerox of your edited copy, or you may copy the editing neatly onto the ribbon copy, holding your rough-edited copy as your insurance copy.] Work in pencil the first time around, you may change your mind.

2. Listen and read. Look for impediments to the flow of the narrative which could be eliminated without loss, that is, superfluous crutch words, false starts, gushings of the interviewer, secondary conversations (the narrator may have been keeping up an off-and-on conversation with someone in the kitchen about the progress of dinner). These may have already been taken care of by an experienced transcriber.

Preserve enough chit-chat to indicate the formality or informality of the interview situation, but condense it, if lengthy, with stage directions, i.e., (Coffee is served. Discussion of mutual acquaintances in the neighborhood.)

3. Check the words and punctuation to be sure they are accurate to the recording. You can catch this by listening, and by knowing

what the narrator is talking about. Watch for mistranscriptions.

4. Note down the need for additional information, such as first names, dates, footnotes to references, definitions of technical, obsolete, or slang terms, and other information you can add editorially. You may add that information as you go, but I suggest you note the need on your transcript and on your notepad and go back and fill that in later. Also note unclear passages which will require clarification by the narrator.

5. Keep a running list of proper names as you go so that you can once and for all check out the correct spelling and then be sure it is the same throughout the transcript. When you have checked the spelling, either in your reference books, or with the narrator, mark it as okay. (Remember that narrators can be wrong, even printed sources like newspapers can be wrong.) Add to your list the spelling you have selected of any special terms used in the interview. For example, an acre-foot of water, agribusiness, Japanese-Americans.

This list should go to the final typist in the event you didn't catch every place the word appeared in the transcript.

6. Editorial style changes. Everyone on the staff should be working with the same accepted style guide, including the transcriber, so matters such as punctuation—use of commas, dashes, dots (elipses), quotation marks, how to write numbers and amounts of money, capitalization, abbreviations, should be in pretty fair order already, but as you read through you will find things to change or question. Capitalization is especially difficult if you are dealing with many government units or official titles of positions. Like your running list of how to spell names and special terms, you may wish to keep a list of how you have decided to capitalize.

Make editorial style changes on the first run-through if you are sure of them, and mark them for further attention if they require some research.

7. Note stories that don't track, are confusing, or places where pieces of the story pop up here and there in the interview in a mixed-up fashion. You may need to do more serious editing here; for repetitions or scattered pieces of a tale, you will have to decide if some should be eliminated or combined, if some should be moved so the

story is all in one piece, or if you should and can lead the researcher to all the segments via the table of contents and the index.

8. Note accounts that you question as to whether they are historically accurate. Perhaps they do not agree with other things you know, or are inconsistent in some way; perhaps they seem partial and need more information before they could be usable. Also note accounts that the narrator seemed reluctant to have released, or that you question if they might not involve slander or contain the possibility of social injury to a person or community. Mark these for further consideration.

9. Prepare a rough table of contents. Jot down on a separate sheet possible chapter and subtitle headings as you go, with the page number. If all has gone well with the interview, these probably follow the interview question outline fairly closely. Chapter headings should serve as a map to the reader so make them substantive, not clever. They may have to serve as an announcement of what the discussion topic is because it may take several pages into the account before it becomes clear to the reader what this is all about. Unlike good expositive writing, oral history interviews do not necessarily begin a new topic with a clear topic sentence. You can do wonders in bringing shape and significance to an interview through the considered wording and placement of headings, but it will probably require several revisions of your first tentative table of contents.

10. When you have finished the first run-through, you should have a transcript that is correct as far as typescript to tape is concerned, has had the simplest deletions made, and is marked as to what needs further close attention. The second reading is to handle all the research questions, and the knotty editorial decisions. At this point, you can put away the tape, but not too far away. You may still need to relisten as you try to rearrange confusing passages and you want to be true to the meaning of the tape.

The Second Reading

This is the hard one, when you solve all the questions that were noted as needing further attention.

11. Additional facts. Use your reference works to check out first names, dates, material for footnotes, etc. and add them if you can. Additional information added by the editor should be in brackets.

12. Unclear accounts. You may be able by close reading and listening, plus your own background research, to figure out what is meant, and to revise the wording slightly to make it clear. Do that, but call the passage to the narrator's attention so she can check to see that this is indeed what she meant.

If you can't make heads or tails of an account, then ask the narrator to straighten it out. But try first; narrators get very upset by garbled accounts, and they may find it difficult to rewrite them, so much so they may postpone ever returning the transcript to you.

13. The unidentified pronoun. One of the most common confusions is due to missing or unclear antecedents. Some people talk in a kind of verbal shorthand which assumes a degree of background and understanding the listener often does not have. A narrator may go on and on with a story about "she" who may be, by turns, grandmother, sister, and daughter, all without a change in antecedent, the "she's" somehow connected in the narrator's mind but the story completely confusing to anyone else. The alert interviewer will keep trying politely to pin down the narrator on who these "hes," "shes," and "theys" are. But when they end up in the transcript, the editor must try to clarify them or the account is valueless.

As an example:

"He always gave us a little spending money. He always wanted to spend it right away because he knew he'd talk him out of it if he didn't."

From previous statements the editor marked it as follows:

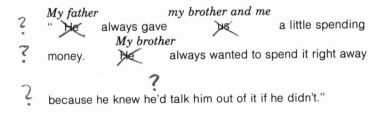

The narrator added "Cousin Bill" for the next to the last "he." In the final typing it was typed without brackets as the additional information had been approved by the narrator and there was no reason to retain the original unclear speech.

If, however, the narrator had not reviewed the transcript, then the editor's clarifications would have been added in brackets to alert the reader that this was only an educated guess.

> "[My father] always gave [my brother and me] a little spending money. [My brother] always wanted to spend it right away because he knew [Cousin Bill] would talk him out of it if he didn't."

14. Partial accounts. These may be accounts that are understandable but which would be more useful with the addition of more details. Ask the narrator an additional question or two in writing, to be answered in writing at the time she reviews the transcript. Mark where the question belongs, type it on a blank page with space for an answer, and insert it in the transcript. Some of those written questions and answers really strike a gusher in terms of valuable information. Don't hesitate to ask for more details. Narrators usually enjoy a second chance to fill in the details.

If the written question was a brief one, and the written answer equally so—for example: "What year was that?" "1921."—there is no point in noting that this tidbit was added after the actual interview. But if the question strikes a two or three-page answer, possibly in a different style (because it will originate as written rather than spoken) and possibly incorporating an update on the topic from the time of the recording, then it should be noted in the final typescript that this was added later, and at what date. For example, to an account recorded before Watergate of the narrator's attendance at the Republican Convention of 1952, the editor had written in the question, "Did you observe Murray Chotiner [Nixon's campaign manager] there, and if so, what was your impression of him?" To this the narrator responded with a five-page critical account of Chotiner. It was important to note the date of the written addition, which came after Watergate and after the publication of several books critical of Chotiner.

15. Bad grammar. This is a touchy editorial decision. The first operating rule is to leave it as is if it is consistent with the way the narrator speaks. Change it if it is obviously just an error of speech arising from thinking while speaking and getting tangled up in a long sentence. The possible contradictory consideration is that the narrator may be very sensitive about what she considers her inadequate speech patterns. You may have a very good idea that if she recognizes one poor grammar construction, she will go through and rewrite the whole thing. It is better for the editor to make a few corrections if it will stave off a full formalization by the narrator. Play it by ear. Aim for the most accurate portrayal of the narrator's speech that you can get away with. Of course, even though you leave the grammar as is, the narrator (or her spouse or child) may go through and correct all the bad grammmer; that is her privilege.

16. Repetitions. Cut out repetitions that have no meaning other than that the interview was conducted over a long period of time and the narrator forget that she had told it already; in the interview history indicate that some repetitions were removed. Leave in repetitions that show emphasis.

Some projects do not believe in removing repetitions, believing they alert the user to the condition of the narrator's memory. I disagree with this point of view. We have found that one of the main things older people are afraid of when they are invited to give an oral history is that they will repeat themselves. Many accept only on condition the interviewer agrees to remove repetitions. Most will not approve a transcript until they or the editor have cleared up repetitions.

I believe it is more considerate to both narrator and eventual user to combine or remove repetitions, and to note that you did this in the interview history. You always have the tape if someone wants to study the condition of the narrator's memory.

17. Rambling questions by the interviewer. This happens more often than you will want to admit, questions that start and stop, backtrack, repeat and fumble. Unless you are trying to document interviewing technique, just pare those questions down to what was finally asked (readers want to know what the narrator has to say, not

the fumblings of the interviewer). But don't change the gist of the question or it will change the meaning of the answer.

18. Question not related to the answer. Occasionally the narrator's answer will have almost no relationship to the question. Most likely this will be a problem of hearing; many people who suffer some hearing loss will answer what they guess the question was rather than ask you to repeat it several times. If it is deafness, then the unrelated answer gives a false picture of the narrator as not quite mentally alert. In that case, it would be advisable to reword your question in such a way as to make it more an open-ended "tell me about 'such-and-such' ". Because probably all the narrator did in fact hear was 'such-and-such' and not what you asked about it. Again, your goal is to preserve the truest portrait of the narrator and a slight alteration of your question may be more accurate than the verbatim question.

The other possibility is that the narrator is trying to sidestep a question. If it's a sidestep, you want to preserve it as a clue to the user. These sorts of decisions require a great sensitivity on the part of the editor to the whole interview situation and to the character of the narrator. This is why I strongly recommend that the interviewer do the editing.

19. Derogatory information. This is a very touchy issue. Occasionally an interview will contain remarks about a person or group which could cause injury to the person mentioned, to the narrator, to the community, or to the oral history program. The narrator may have been worried about the remarks and may have told the interviewer she will consider deleting them, or she may be totally unaware that they could be damaging, or she may be downright spiteful. The remarks may be true or false, and you may not know. In any event, you suspect you have an explosive situation here.

First, is the information of any historical significance? Is it necessary to know who the person was, or would an anonymous 'they' do just as well for the sense of the story? If it is of no significance, edit the passage to generalize it, and call the rewrite to the narrator's attention for her approval.

But if it is of significance, and often it is, call it to the narrator's attention, and suggest that certain passages be placed under seal for a suitable period of time. Don't suggest sealing the whole interview, only the necessary number of pages.

A third alternative is to let it stand and prepare for the big storm. But in most instances, the important stories will have been carefully censored by your narrators before they speak, or they will insist on seal privileges, while only the little personal items will remain.

In any event, think carefully, discuss with the rest of the staff, and be aware of what you are getting into. And do call the sensitive passages to the attention of the narrator. It would be a breach of your responsibility to the narrator to allow something to be said in the warmth of your good rapport, and then to let it slip by unnoticed by the narrator in the review.

20. Adding chapter headings and subtitles. Now that you have taken a detailed overview of the entire transcript, review your tentative headings and decide if they are adequate. Reword them if necessary. I would recommend rather broad chapter headings, with dates: For example, "Growing Up in Butte, Montana, 1898–1918"; "Medical Training in Philadelphia, 1919–1925"; etc. Chapters could be about 20–40 pages. Chapters should be broken down into subheadings, and depending on content, into sub-subheadings.

Usually a major topic heading will coincide with an interview session because a valid way to interview is to take up one major topic per interview session. But this is not always the case (the first interview may have run over a little past childhood and into medical education). Indicate the interview dates and when one session ends and the next begins in the transcript, but don't feel obliged to make the chapters conform to the interview sessions.

It is nice to have balanced chapters and subchapters, all of about equal pages, but it won't necessarily come out that way. You may end up with a 50-page chapter followed by a 10-page chapter; a 9-page subchapter followed by a half-page subchapter. Don't worry. You are working with given material, not with material you are writing yourself. Aim for logical, helpful headings, and congratulate yourself if they come out moderately well balanced as well.

Preparing the Transcript for the Narrator's Review

21. Neatly write in editorial changes, titles, etc. You may be copying your pencilled editing of a carbon copy onto the ribbon copy in ink. Or you may be inking in the changes you had previously pencilled on the ribbon copy prior to xeroxing the whole thing.

Put question marks in the margin wherever you want the narrator to pay special attention.

22. Prepare a list of questions for the narrator by page number. For example: p. 2—Lizt, is this name spelled correctly? p. 3—does this paragraph read correctly? p. 18—can you add the date here? p. 20—do you remember your professor's name? p. 24—would you add several paragraphs on this point (questions and blank paper included in transcript at the appropriate point). p. 52—would you add a few paragraphs about your children and grandchildren, etc.

While you can never be sure how carefully narrators will read through the transcript, they almost all go over that list of questions to check and will respond to them, either in the transcript on the proper page, or on the question list.

23. Type up a table of contents with page numbers, tentative title for the interview (the narrator may have some comments on the title), proposed illustrations and where they would go. All of these not only permit the narrator to participate in the putting together of the total interview, but they also make the rough transcript look like something more than a bundle of marked-up typewritten pages. A narrator will pay careful attention to a neat transcript with a table of contents, question list, and illustration list.

[Dr. Edward Kellogg]

Doe: She was the wife of E.K. Strong, you know, of Stanford who

developed those tests, Stanford Aptitude tests.

Jones: Stanford-Binet tests?

Doe: Yes. I remember one night when there was a great turmoil
        in one of our colleges
        about someone who was supposed to be a Communist or con-
        way
        nected in some ~~with~~/with them. ~~In one of our colleges.~~ People

wanted to get him out, and no one could find anything about

him. I think there were twenty-five pages of ~~legal size~~ onionskin

paper—legal size—that Mrs. Strong and I went over and read
        d
until two or three o'clock the morning, and we couldn't fine one

thing against the man. Well! And this was the kind of thing that
        witch
went on—~~with~~ hunting went on for a long time.

Fig. 4. An example of simple editing.

Doe: While I was still in high school I served as chairman of the
        —Dawes
        finance committee of the Coolidge-~~Dolls~~-Republican Club.

Coolidge - Dawes

*Fig. 5. A mistranscription, caught by the interviewer who realized that
Coolidge's running mate was Charles G. Dawes. Otherwise, this was impossible to hear, and the narrator died before checking the transcript.*

Doe: And we went down there to Stanford. And we bought some of that
       Army stuff—after the war—plastics. Rain—you never saw it rain so
       hard in your life. And those things just disintegrated. We got wringing
       wet. On the way back, we stopped at a restaurant on El Camino
       Real, at a place there where Warren used to like to eat. He
       always maintained a change of clothes in a locker there. So he
       changed his wet clothes there.

Doe: And we went down there to Stanford. Rain—you never saw it rain so
       hard in your life. And we bought some of that Army stuff—after the
       war—plastics. And those things just disintegrated. We got wringing
       wet. On the way back, we stopped at a restaurant on El Camino Real,
       at a place there where Warren used to like to eat. He always main-
       tained a change of clothes in a locker there. So he changed his wet
       clothes there.

Fig. 6. An example of changing sentence order for clarity.

Jones: I think the *Tribune* supported Warren even before that, didn't they?

Doe: Yes, they had supported him. They had supported him in his election campaigns in California for district attorney.

Jones: Could you give me some idea of the relationship ~~between the *Trib* and . . . I mean, I would like to get a picture of the "on the ground" workings between~~ Earl Warren and the *Tribune* when he was D.A. ? ~~because~~ This would help ~~indicate to~~ us ~~how to~~ evaluate the various clippings that we read. ~~For instance, there are several clipping books which Earl Warren's office kept, and this includes clippings from several different newspapers. One of the really rough jobs that we are having right now, is trying to evaluate this as source material from the various newspapers.~~ I had been told by some people that ~~Warren frequently would . . . that he had had a very good working relation-ship with *Tribune* reporters. In other words, that they would . . . like you do when you have a good relationship . . .~~ *Tribune* ~~the~~ reporters would hold stories if it was necessary for a couple of days when ~~he~~ *Warren* was in a hot case, ~~or investigating~~ or something. ~~And they would cooperate with him to that extent, and~~ In return, ~~he~~ *Warren* would try to give them as full an account as possible. Do you know anything about this?

Doe: No, I can't say that I could do that. I do know that Warren from his earliest days had a good relationship with the press in general and I'm quite sure that he would never have gotten himself in the position that one paper could feel that the other one was being favored on stories or breaking stories.

Fig. 7. An example of a question that is too long and unclear. Cut it down to its essence.

Jones: I think the *Tribune* supported Warren even before that, didn't they?

Doe: Yes, they had supported him. They had supported him in his election campaigns in California for district attorney.

Jones: Could you give me some idea of the relationship between Earl Warren and the *Tribune* when he was D.A.? This would help us evaluate the various clippings that we read. I had been told by some people that *Tribune* reporters would hold stories if it was necessary for a couple of days when Warren was in a hot case or something. In return, Warren would try to give them as full an account as possible. Do you know anything about this?

Doe: No, I can't say that I could do that. I do know that Warren from his earliest days had a good relationship with the press in general and I'm quite sure that he would never have gotten himself in the position that one paper could feel that the other one was being favored on stories or breaking stories.

Fig. 8. The question used in Fig. 7, after it has been shortened.

Insert later

Jones: And where did you meet your ~~first~~ *second* wife?, Mary?

Doe: In I guess San Francisco, but I didn't marry her until I got to France. See how women chase me?

Jones: *Where did you meet* Your first wife?

Doe: ~~Oh, my first wife!~~ I went out to dinner one night at an ectodontist's house.

~~Jones: At a who?~~

~~Doe: At an ectodontist's home.~~

Jones: What is that?

Doe: He's a guy who pulls teeth for a living.

Jones: Ectodontist?

Doe: "Ect" meaning "out," and "Donto," meaning "teeth."

~~Jones: I never heard that word before.~~

Doe: He's a tooth-outer! ~~What?~~

~~Jones: I said I never heard that word before.~~

Doe: That's a specialist. I met her at his house, and married her in San Francisco. She died ten years later, I guess.

Jones: And you had one daughter.

She was born in Sacramento.

Doe: Yes. She's married with 2 young daughters, in San Francisco. *She and her husband* ~~They~~ just got divorced. ~~They just got divorced, and she is having an affair with a guy who's the director of personnel at~~ ABC. ~~Yes, that's the~~ right name.

Fig. 9. An example of an interview that needs much editing due to speaking and hearing problems.

Jones: ~~Excuse me, I didn't understand you. What kind of a fair? African?~~

Doe: ~~[Patiently] No, an affair. They sleep together.~~

Jones: ~~Oh, come on now. I know what you're getting at. I didn't know what your word was in between there.~~ What was her married name, before she was divorced?

Doe: ~~_____.~~

Jones: ~~What was that again?~~

Doe: ~~_____.~~

Jones: ~~I didn't catch that.~~

Doe: ~~Smith! S-M-Y-T-H-E.~~

Jones: ~~Oh, Smith. Did you say with a "y" or an "i"?~~

Doe: ~~"Y". Like yellow dog.~~ Mrs. George ~~Smith~~ *Smythe*. She has ~~2~~ *two* boys.

Jones: ~~Dr. Doe, could I ask you to put your teeth in? I think That it might make things a little clearer if you do.~~

Doe: ~~Oh, yes.~~

Jones: ~~Here's the cup.~~

Doe: ~~I'm sorry.~~

Jones: ~~Oh, don't be sorry, and then I won't be sorry that I was bold enough to ask.~~

Doe: ~~That's the way to do it. Maybe that's better now.~~

Jones: ~~I think so. All right?~~

check. Is it two sons or two daughters?

Fig. 9 (Continued).

Doe: All right.

Jones: I want to go back to Sacramento with you.

Doe: All right! Have you been in Sacramento?

Jones: Yes, I spent a year there.

Doe: When was that?

Jones: About 1954. Before they put in the new freeway.

Doe: That really speeds up the traffic.

Jones: You've told me about how you met your second wife, Mary.

Insert *

Doe: I knew her family in Sacramento.

Jones: How big a family is it?

Her mother

Doe: She had five girls and one boy. Her husband was dead. Her

mother was alive, and that was it.

Jones: Of course you met her brother in France?

Doe: Yes.

Jones: His name was Lawson, was it?

Doe: Lewison. Also her father's name. My daughter was born in

Sacramento.

Jones: Why did you and Mary decide to go to France?

Doe: Her brother wanted us to come.

Fig. 9 (Continued).

Jones: Where did you meet your first wife?

Doe: I went out to dinner one night at an ectodontist's house.

Jones: What is that?

Doe: He's a guy who pulls teeth for a living.

Jones: Ectodontist?

Doe: "Ect" meaning "out," and "donto," meaning "teeth." He's a tooth-outer! That's a specialist. I met her at his house, and married her in San Francisco. She died ten years later, I guess.

Jones: And you had one daughter.

Doe: Yes. She was born in Sacramento. She's married with two young daughters, in San Francisco. She and her husband just got divorced.

Jones: What was her married name, before she was divorced?

Doe: Mrs. George Smythe. She has two daughters.

Jones: And where did you meet your second wife, Mary?

Doe: In I guess San Francisco, but I didn't marry her until I got to France. See how women chase me? I knew her family in Sacramento.

Jones: How big a family is it?

Doe: Her mother had five girls and one boy. Her husband was dead. Her mother was alive, and that was it.

Jones: Of course. You met her brother in France?

Doe: Yes.

Jones: His name was Lawson, was it?

Doe: Lewison. Also her father's name.

Jones: Why did you and Mary decide to go to France?

Doe: Her brother wanted us to come.

Fig. 9A. The finished transcript.

Doe: What I'm going to do, ~~I'm going to let you—I have some copies~~ here of the book ~~to read, because~~ I think we've cap- *is let you read this* *were writing on streetwork in the ghetto.* * tured a lot of the history and some of the things that are so good in this, ~~that I would like for you—and I know it won't take you long—and then I'd like for you to send it back to me.~~

Mr. Doe, is there another title for this?

Jones: I'd really like the opportunity to read it. I'd consider that a privilege.

No.

Doe: And it's the first ten chapters, and I hope that once you do this that if you run across anybody that would help us in trying to get this out, because I think that what's here—we spent a lot of time, about two years, compiling this, even before I left. There are a lot of things in there that we still want to say in the other chapters. Like I say, I haven't sent this to Bill, but I do believe that you would really enjoy this because we spent a lot time in trying to—I talked to Ed a lot and gave him my inner thoughts. For the last fourteen years, I think I've talked to Ed daily, almost, throughout all the crises. So a lot of the things that he has recorded are quite true and even some of the things I had forgotten, because he was writing them down at that time.

Doe: *We spent about two years compling these first ten chapters, even before I left. There are a lot of things we still want to say, and we're now looking for some help in getting it published.*

   For the last fourteen years, I've talked to Ed Hammond daily, almost, and given him my inner thoughts, throughout all the crises. So what he's written is quite true, even some things that I had forgotten, because he was writing them down all the time.

Fig. 10. Editing for clarity, to cut out fumbles and get a clear statement.

* A History of streetwork in the ghetto, Ed Hammond, manuscript in process, Oakland, 1974

Doe: What I'm going to do is let you read this copy of the book we're writing on streetwork in the ghetto.* I think we've captured a lot of the history and some of the things that are so good in this.

Jones: I'd really like the opportunity to read it. I'd consider that a privilege.

Doe: We spent about two years compiling these first ten chapters, even before I left. There are a lot of things we still want to say, and we're now looking for some help in getting it published.

   For the last fourteen years, I've talked to Ed Hammond daily, almost, and given him my inner thoughts, throughout all the crises. So what he's written is quite true, even some things that I had forgotten, because he was writing them down all the time.

*A History of Streetwork in the Ghetto, Ed Hammond, manuscript in process, Oakland, 1974.

Fig. 11. The material in Fig. 10, after editing for clarity.

Jones: Did you definitely go out and hunt for people?

Doe: Oh yes. We advertised for Nixon, you know.

Jones: Oh, ~~you told me that.~~ *yes. We want that in the record.* ~~I wanted you to put it on the tape too.~~ This was after he came back from the war?

Doe: That's right. Well. Gee, the names escape me now, but there was ~~the~~ *this* congressman over there in the Whittier district.

~~Jones: He'll be in the blue book.~~

~~Doe: Yes. The one that Nixon defeated.~~ He was a great New Dealer.

~~Jones: Oh. Oh, of course. I know who you mean.~~

Doe: His father was head of a school over there.

~~Jones: I'll think of it in a minute, if you don't. Okay?~~

Fig. 12. Adding a written question. The editor added this query in order to get further details. In this instance, the interviewee did not add any more information, so the question was removed from the final transcript.

Doe: *Jerry* ~~Voorhis~~ Voorhis. But he was pretty well entrenched. *¶* We were told to try to find somebody, so there was nobody that wanted to run. They asked me to run. They asked a lot of other people to run, but they wouldn't go.

Jones: Why didn't you run?

Doe: Oh, I was never interested in holding office.

Jones: Who else did they ask?

Doe: Oh, I can't say for sure. I think there was a lawyer out in Alhambra named Krusi, ~~who either~~ wanted to run, ~~or~~—. I visualize some of the others, but I forget. Anyway, we held meetings and couldn't decide on anybody, so somebody said, "Let's advertise." So we put an advertisement in the papers out there in the San Gabriel Valley. I don't have a copy of it; ~~but~~—. I didn't attend to that, but a lawyer in San Marino whose name I've also forgotten— can visualize him *too.* ~~very well~~ ~~did~~. It said, "Wanted: man to run for office. Must be a veteran, young, ambitious, hard-working/—". The usual stuff. And Nixon was one who thought he might run.

Jones: What did you do? Did *your* ~~the~~ CRA group interview these candidates?

Question: Other scholars, such as a biographer of Voorhis, have said that there is great difficulty in finding evidence to support the story of the want ad. Can you give us any specific information, such as the name of the paper, a description of the ad, who placed it? Now that Richard Nixon is president, it becomes a very important story. Any further leads will be appreciated.

Can you add any names here now

Fig. 12 (Continued).

Jones: Did you definitely go out and hunt for people?

Doe: Oh yes. We advertised for Nixon, you know.

Jones: Oh, yes. We want that in the record. This was after he came back from the war?

Doe: That's right. Well. Gee, the names escape me now, but there was this congressman over there in the Whittier district. He was a great New Dealer. His father was head of a school over there. Jerry Voorhis. But he was pretty well entrenched.

       We were told to try to find somebody, so there was nobody that wanted to run. They asked me to run. They asked a lot of other people to run, but they wouldn't go.

Jones: Why didn't you run?

Doe: Oh, I was never interested in holding office.

Jones: Who else did they ask?

Doe: Oh, I can't say for sure. I think there was a lawyer out in Alhambra named Krusi, who wanted to run. I visualize some of the others, but I forget. Anyway, we held meetings and couldn't decide on anybody, so somebody said, "Let's advertise." So we put an advertisement in the papers out there in the San Gabriel Valley. I don't have a copy of it; I didn't attend to that, but a lawyer in San Marino whose name I've also forgotten—I can visualize him too. It said, "Wanted: man to run for office. Must be a veteran, young, ambitious, hard-working—". The usual stuff.* And Nixon was one who thought he might run.

Jones: What did you do? Did your CRA group interview these candidates?

----

*This want ad is quoted in David Wallenchinsky, *The People's Almanac*, 1975, p. 318. But no copy of the ad has been located by the Regional Oral History Office so far. Editor.

Fig. 13. The final version of the transcript shown in Fig. 12.

Jones: Is this what John meant when he said the building was going

to create a bloody mess?

Doe: Oh, yes. There was a lot jealousy. You had some of the board

members who were quite frightened about where was it

going: and Mr. Smith, they'd never really met him. He

wouldn't come to a board meeting, and this type of thing. You

had some business people on there, and you had a Mr. Roe,

who was a very fine person whose given a lot of time to the

community, but who really wants to be loved and loved and

loved to death, and it's really too bad. A very fine person,

very bright, and at one time we were quite close, and then

this thing with Bill came down. He listened to some lies and

he was carried away by some of them. He just felt that I had to

go.

Jones: Is this what John meant when he said the building was going
to create a bloody mess?

Doe: Oh, yes. There was a lot of jealousy. You had some of the
board members who were quite frightened about where was
it going. They'd never really met Mr. Smith; he wouldn't
come to a board meeting, and this type of thing. You had
some business people on the board, very fine people who've
given a lot of time to the community, but with their own
personal hangups, and it's really too bad. Very fine people,
very bright, and at one time we were quite close, and then
this thing with Bill came down, and some of them were
carried away by it and just felt that I had to go.

Fig. 14. Softening a derogatory remark.

Fry: Well, start over and tell me from the beginning about that; how the whole thing came up.

Vernon: Well, we were in jail only two nights, I guess, three days, that would be two nights, wouldn't it? And the second night somehow one of the girls, could we be allowed to go into the corridor. There was a corridor right outside the cells, and it wasn't a very forbidding place, and she asked the matron if we could be allowed to have some music on the organ, and the girls asked us. And so she said, "Can anybody here play the organ?" And I said I could play hymns a little bit. So the matron said that would be all right. And the girls went out of their cells. They were mostly black as I remember, and then they said ask Evelyn what she would like. And I asked, "What would you like me to play?" And they said, "Ask Evelyn." Evelyn was a quiet girl who was there for drug addiction, I think. And we asked Evelyn, and she said, "God be with you until we meet again." So we proceeded to sing "God be with you until we meet again."

And just as we were in the midst of it, the door opened into the main part of the jail, and the warden came in with a newspaper man. He was a Hearst man. And I know a little while later I had a letter from Mrs. [William] Kent in Kentfield. [Elizabeth]—Do you know where Kentfield is? Right. [California] at the foot of Mt. Tamalpais.

Fry: Yes.

Vernon: I had a letter from Mrs. Kent in Kentfield enclosing the column from the Hearst paper, I guess it was the *Herald*, was it?

Fig. 15. A difficult transcript. The editor had to listen several times to catch missing portions, and then revise slightly for clarity. A transcript with so many corrections on it should be retyped before submitting it to the narrator.

Fry: Well, start over and tell me from the beginning about that; how the whole thing came up.

Vernon: Well, we were in jail only two nights, I guess, three days, that would be two nights, wouldn't it? And the second night one of the girls among the inmates already there asked the matron if we could be allowed to go into the corridor. There was a corridor right outside the cells, and it wasn't a very forbidding place. She asked the matron if we could be allowed to have some music on the organ, and the matron said she thought so. And so the girls asked us, "Can anybody here play the organ?" And I said I could play hymns a little bit. So the matron said that would be all right. And the girls went out of their cells. They were mostly black as I remember, and I asked, "What would you like me to play?" And they said, "Ask Evelyn what she would like." Evelyn was a quiet girl who was there for drug addiction, I think. And we asked Evelyn, and she said, "God Be With You Until We Meet Again." So we proceeded to sing "God Be With You Until We Meet Again."

And just as we were in the midst of it, the door opened into the main part of the jail, and the warden came in with a newspaper man. He was a Hearst man. And I know a little while later I had a letter from Mrs. [William] Kent [Elizabeth] in Kentfield [California]—do you know where Kentfield is? Right at the foot of Mt. Tamalpais.

Fry: Yes.

Vernon: I had a letter from Mrs. Kent in Kentfield enclosing the column from the Hearst paper, I guess it was the *Herald*, was it?

Fig. 16. The corrected, retyped transcript after editing.

8

The Narrator's Review
and Approval

We come now to the most crucial step in the oral history process, next to the interview itself, and that is submitting the transcript to the narrator and getting her final approval to use it. If you fail here, you will have nothing to show for the project's investment in research, taping, and typing time. Also, it is at this step that you have a final chance to check the historical authenticity of your interview, and to get any additional information that your narrator can provide.

This is a step that requires paying personal attention to each transcript and each narrator; some projects end up with as much as 50% nonreturns of transcripts because they make this a routine clerical step. The return of the transcript should be handled by the interviewer if he is a long-term person with the project, if not, by the director. In any event, the director should be introduced to the narrator, either by letter, telephone, or in person so that if the interviewer should leave before all details are completed, there is someone known to the narrator who can finish up.

Steps in Returning the Transcript

1. Prepare the transcript neatly, with chapter headings inserted; with a table of contents, and with a draft title page. The more the transcript looks like something substantial, the more the narrator will be inclined to treat it seriously and not just as a bundle of papers to be looked over some day.

2. Indicate questions you have for the narrator in the margin with a question mark—either brief questions such as the spelling of a name, or lengthy questions to which you hope the narrator will respond with a sentence, paragraph, or page of further explanation. But in addition, add a page that lists all your major queries and the page number on which they appear—some narrators will thumb rapidly through the transcript, but will respond to the questions on a special page.

Keep a xerox copy of the edited transcript plus all your editorial questions, just in case the narrator loses her copy. We hold these copies in our "Insurance Copy File" until the transcript is returned from the narrator with her approval.

3. Write a personal letter explaining what you want the narrator to do. In your letter mention some special information she has contributed, explain what you want done in the way of correcting the transcript, be sure to urge the narrator not to formalize her manner of speaking, explain (again) what you are going to do with the transcript after she returns it, and leave the door open for her questions.

4. Deliver the transcript with a personal touch. If it will be by mail, telephone first to check the address or whether the narrator will be in town. If delivered in person, include the letter with the transcript even though you explain personally what should be done. The narrator will wish to reread the letter as she corrects.

If the transcript is especially long, the result of several interview sessions, you will need to consider carefully whether it would be easier for the narrator to receive and review it a chapter at a time, or whether she would prefer to have it all at once.

5. Call again in a week or so to find out how the review is going. Don't be a pest but don't let yourself be forgotten either.

Fig. 17 shows a sample letter.

Why Narrators Don't Return Transcripts

For the most part, your narrators will be happy to correct and return the transcript promptly, and will look forward eagerly to receiving from your project their copy of the completed manuscript. But there will always be a few who will be slow, or reluctant, or who

SAMPLE LETTER

Oral History Project
Central City Library
Sixth & Main Streets
Central City, California 95867

1 July 1976

Mrs. Robert T. Hale
1220 Spruce Street
Central City, California 95867

Dear Mrs. Hale:

Here is the transcript of the interview we tape recorded in April, ready for you to look over and approve for final typing. Your account of the demolition and rebuilding of Oxford School and all of the attendant debates while you were on the School Board will be especially useful to researchers. We are also pleased to have your account of the difficulties of running a household during the Depression.

I enclose a sheet with the suggested title and list of headings. How do you want your name on the title page, Mrs. Robert T. Hale or Mary McKinnon Hale? Also enclosed is a sheet with a list of questions about portions of the transcript that need either your careful checking or about which we would like more details. Please answer the queries on it.

The manuscript as corrected by you and returned to us will be the draft from which we will type final copies. One of the final bound copies will go to you, one to the History Room, Gold Town Library at Gold Town and one will be retained in our library. The library copies will be open to patrons to read on the library premises. Other libraries in the area may also request copies.

We would like to include a picture of you. If you could choose one or two recent (or older) photographs you like, we could have them copied and return them to you.

Thank you for the time that you have put in so far, and for the checking that lies ahead. I hope that you and Mr. Hale are keeping well.

Sincerely yours,

Mary Fontenrose
Interviewer

P.S. Please call me if you have any questions, 642-7395

Enclosure

Fig. 17. A sample letter.

will require a great deal of follow-up time. Never give up (unless it is a poor transcript that you can afford to lose anyhow), but accept the fact that you will have a few failures. Some projects insert a stipulation that if the transcript is not returned within a specific time, the copy will be assumed to be acceptable.

For the slow returns, try to figure out what the problem is and what you can do about it. Most narrators will fall into the following categories:

1. *Narrators who don't understand what they are expected to do,* or the correcting is difficult for them. It may be that they have difficulty reading or writing—the infirmities of age or illness can make what was once a small task pretty overwhelming. In such cases, you will probably have to make another visit, explain again, perhaps read the transcript or the questionable portions of it to them and write down any corrections yourself, or if lengthy additions, record them and add them to the transcript.

Another alternative is to enlist the aid of a family member to do this. Be cautious in this approach. Sometimes a spouse or son or daughter will be far more insistent than the narrator on cleaning up and formalizing the transcript and you may end up with an emasculated version of what was originally a lively tale. On the other hand, a family member may be very helpful in checking records for dates and names, and in helping the narrator to remember key or interesting events.

2. *Narrators who are too busy.* Often narrators still carry a full share of community, social, family, or job commitments. In a few cases, they may know their days are numbered and they have other priorities before the review of their transcript. There is not much you can do in these cases except, perhaps, offer to simplify the job by doing all the fine editing yourself, following their instructions, and only referring the few most difficult questions to them. You may just have to wait until they do have time. In any event, be sure you have the legal release signed.

3. *Narrators who don't want to end the process.* The interview process is usually a satisfying one to narrators, they look forward to continued contact with their interviewer, and as the process nears its end, they find reason to fiddle and dawdle.

You may have continuing tasks for them to do after they complete the transcript. One such task is to prepare a family tree, going as far backwards and forwards as they can. In our office, we have prepared family tree forms which are a little simpler than the usual genealogical forms and these are given to the narrators after their review is completed. Some narrators enjoy working on a family tree form; others feel it is a foolish vanity and refuse. The filled-out family tree can be part of the appendix of their interview, or can be filed separately in a genealogy file. Other tasks may be finding appropriate photographs or illustrative pages to add to the interview or related papers.

There should be a deadline for every interviewing series, both for the purpose of setting up time schedules, and for the morale of the staff and the narrators, and often for reasons of budget (most public and grant funds have cut-off dates). If there is not a real deadline, set yourselves one such as a special celebration when the interviews will be presented (usually a historical date), a publication date for a booklet of excerpts, a reception for participants, a progress report to the funding agency, etc. Dawdling narrators can be hurried along to meet this deadline. Don't be so rigid that if they miss the deadline, their transcript cannot be accessioned for next year's deadline.

Retrieving the Transcript

Unless distance is a factor, try to pick up the transcript in person at an agreed-upon date. A personal pick-up appointment will hurry the narrator along, you will not face the delay of the narrator having to go to the post office to have the package weighed and stamped, there is no danger of loss in the mails, and most importantly, you can settle any other matters that are still pending.

If you have not already done so, this is the time to get a signed legal agreement. And at this point, if not previously, collect such photographs and other illustrative material as you may wish to use with the interview transcript. You may have to copy and return precious family photographs so gauge your requests to your budget. Discuss the question of the narrator's papers and memorabilia; you can leave the final arrangements until a later date if they require further thought or if you wish to prolong the relationship with the narrator. The papers, if any, may or may not be useful; they may be or may not be appropriate to your institution (suitable for the University's department of special collections, not suitable for the community college library). You may be authorized to decide or you may need to refer the collecting to a librarian.

If the papers appear valuable but not appropriate to your institution, give the narrator your best advice as to an appropriate repository, and inform that repository of the papers. Whatever the final decision, a copy of the interview transcript should go with the papers, and conversely, the interview transcript should include information on where the narrator's papers may be found.

Within a week, send a letter thanking the narrator for her review work, indicate what you will do next, and let the narrator know about when she may expect her final copy.

The Case for Not Submitting the Transcript for Approval

The foregoing sections on the narrator's review and approval of the transcript have been written on the premise that your oral history program is a community project, that it deals primarily with historical events, persons, and places (i.e., more public, such as education in a one-room schoolhouse; less personal, for example, not a study of birth control methods in the early 1900s). One assumes that the interviews will be available under the name of the narrator and that quotations from the interview will be attributed to the narrator, and that the narrators comprise a fairly literate group. This is not the case for all oral history programs, and there are instances when it would be unrealistic and counter-productive to expect narrators to review their transcripts.

Some projects may seek very personal and familial data for sociological sorts of studies. While this material may be transcribed for easy use, it is seldom intended to be used by the public, and the names of the narrators are usually coded so that no quotations can be traced back to the narrator. It would not be feasible to ask narrators to review and approve the transcripts of such interviews; neither would it be wise to have such a project conducted by a community-based, volunteer oral history program, such as this booklet is designed to serve.

However, it would be possible to have a community oral history program that records a group of persons who may be verbally skilled, but not accustomed to dealing with written statements. To try to reduce their narrations to the typed page and then to ask them to approve it would be futile. It would be wiser to explain the intended uses very clearly on the tape, then to check with them at the end of the interview as to whether you may use the material, again on the tape, and to accept that oral approval as satisfactory. You might offer to play the tape back, then or later, if it seems appropriate. You should still get a signed written release.

The public use of transcripts prepared from such tapes requires more judgment than the use of narrator-approved transcripts. Because the transcripts will not have been checked for accuracy by the narrator, it is essential that they be carefully checked against the tape by the oral history staff. Even if they are accurate renditions of the spoken word, they may contain the sorts of errors that pass in spoken language but which would have been caught if the narrator had read them over. Or the transcript, though accurate as to fact, may in writing appear so colloquial that the narrator or her family will be offended if they see it in print. So be especially careful in using any unreviewed transcripts.

Some projects have chosen not to submit transcripts for approval because the narrator or her family may "sanitize"' the material, i.e., clean it up in fact or in presentation. I feel this is a self-defeating approach. The dissatisfaction of a few narrators may do more damage to the history-gathering goals of the program than the loss of a few juicy facts or examples of earthy language. I would recommend that narrators be allowed to revise their transcripts if they wish; the oral history program having equal rights to try to persuade them not to delete or formalize. A suitable compromise would be to produce an approved transcript, but to get permission to keep and play the tapes exactly as spoken.

9

Legal Agreements

Inasmuch as the whole purpose of an oral history program is to make the information that is captured in the interviews available to many users (not just to the interviewer), it is important that this availability be insured by having the narrator sign a release to the information, and to do that as soon after the recording of the interview as possible.

The narrator should be made aware of this purpose before she agrees to be interviewed. This purpose should be spelled out clearly in a letter to the narrator, even though it has been explained in person; this way she can read it over again before the interview, and the project will have evidence in its files that it was clearly explained. Not only is this fair to the narrator, but it also establishes a strong presumption that this is what the narrator intended, even though she may fail to sign an agreement. However, try to get an agreement in writing so you don't have to lean on strong presumptions.

It is more effective to get a general release at the close of the interview so that you can safely proceed with processing and be assured of the usability of the interview should the narrator die before it is ready for her to approve. But the narrator should be guaranteed the privilege of adding restrictions later, should she wish to do so. Most narrators will not want to add restrictions, but that guarantee is essential if you expect to get a candid interview and if you expect the narrator to sign a general release at the close of the interview session.

The legal agreement should be as short and simple as possible. It should open the interview tape and transcript to research, educational uses, and to quotation and publication in part or in full. The ownership and administration of the interview should be turned over to an official of an institution that will be around to administer it in perpetuity. While this may be your oral history program, it may also be a public library or other larger institution.

Figures 18 and 19 show short, simple agreements which will be adequate for most interviews. We use this for all but lengthy biographical memoirs in which the narrator may feel a more proprietary interest. For those we have a longer agreement, sprinkled with more legal verbiage, but essentially the same except that it grants to the narrator the right to edit before publication of quotations, if she so wishes.

Restrictions

There may be instances in which the narrator will wish to restrict the use of the interview, perhaps for a certain number of years, perhaps to research only by persons the narrator approves (she probably means scholars can read it but not the neighbors), perhaps to publication only with the narrator's permission. In each instance, the appropriate restriction can be added to the simple agreement, and I include some attorney-approved clauses you can use. (See Fig. 20).

A few interviews may include accounts of long-forgotten tales of scandal or incompetence or sharp business practices that could be either actionable as slander, libel, or invasion of privacy, or could reactivate community feuds. Though the danger of libel suits is rather remote, the oral history program has some responsibility to avoid "social injury," especially at the local or family level. So the project director or interviewer may wish to counsel the narrator to place restrictions on certain passages. Failing that, I recommend retaining in principle the right to place library-imposed restrictions on oral history materials, and that right is incorporated in the sample legal agreement. Such restrictions should only be in the interests of preventing social injury, never in the interests of giving some preferred scholar or group priority rights on use.

If the narrator or the oral history program wants restrictions, then they should be worked out so as to include only the sensitive material, and so as to be easy to administer. It would be a waste to close an entire interview for twenty years just because it includes five minutes of comments that might hurt someone's feelings. Close the sensitive transcript pages, erase those passages from the patron-use tape and close the archival master tape, but leave the rest of the interview open to research.

The sensitive passages should be closed for a specified number of years, usually until the date when it may reasonably be expected all the participants will be deceased. Don't leave it at a vague date such as "five years after the death of so-and-so" unless you think the depository where the interviews will go has sufficient staff to assign someone to permanent obituary watching.

In the case where the narrator wishes to have a say in who reads the interview, or what is quoted, set up the restriction in such a way that you notify the narrator at her last reported address and give her time to say "no" before you grant permission. Otherwise you may find the use of the interview stymied in this age of the mobile elderly, simply because the narrator has moved and failed to notify you of her new address.

Whether to Copyright or Not

Copyright provides some protection against having the interview quoted without permission. It may also discourage users from quoting the interview, and the whole purpose of the oral history program is to encourage use. I would suggest that if you are certain that there will be a quick, efficient, and reasonable administration of the interviews wherever they are deposited, you copyright in the name of the depository. But if that depository has a considerable turn-over of staff, or it is staffed by nervous Nellies or the kind of librarians who feel manuscripts are to be owned, guarded, and preserved but not used, then protect your stake in the wide use of your interviews by marking them open for research, open for publication. (Of course, there is no foolproof way to foresee how your interviews will be administered in perpetuity.)

If you do decide to copyright, just put the copyright symbol [©] on the title page, front or back, with the date. It is not necessary to file a copyright form and send in your $10 and two copies of the interview. If your claim is infringed upon, you can file retroactively to your date of "publication."

The Bancroft Library
University of California

Regional Oral History Office   Berkeley, California 94720

I, _____, do hereby give to The Bancroft Library for such
<small>name</small>
scholarly and educational uses as the Director of The Bancroft Library shall determine the following tape-recorded interview(s) recorded with me on _____ for The Bancroft Library as an unrestricted gift and
<small>date(s)</small>
transfer to the University of California legal title and all literary property rights including copyright. This gift does not preclude any use which I may want to make of the information in the recordings myself.

This agreement may be revised or amended by mutual consent of the parties undersigned.

_____
Signature

_____

_____
Name & address of interviewee

_____
Date

_____
Department Head
Regional Oral History Office
The Bancroft Library

_____
Date

Subject of Interview(s)_____

Fig. 18. A sample legal agreement.

Donated Tapes Collection
Regional Oral History Office

The Bancroft Library
University of California
Berkeley, California 94720

We, _____ and_____, do hereby give to
      Narrator   *Interviewer*

The Bancroft Library for such scholarly and educational uses as the Director of
The Bancroft Library shall determine the following tape-recorded interview(s)
recorded on _____ as an unrestricted gift and transfer to the Univer-
             dates(s)

sity of California legal title and all literary property rights including copyright.
This gift does not preclude any use which we may want to make of the information in the recordings ourselves.

_____

Signature of Narrator

_____

_____

_____

_____

Name & Address of Narrator

Accepted for The Bancroft Library by _____

_____
Dated

_____
Department Head
Regional Oral History Office

_____
Dated

_____

Signature of Interviewer

_____

_____

_____

Name & Address of Interviewer

_____

Dated

_____
Subject of Interview(s)

Fig. 19. A legal agreement covering gift by both narrator and interviewer.

POSSIBLE EXCEPTIONS TO ROHO SHORT FORM

Closed, Total Interview

Except that the entire tape and transcript shall be closed to all users until _____
date

Except that the parties hereto agree that the entire tape and transcript shall not be made available to anyone other than the parties hereto until _____
date

Closed, Except With Permission

The interview tape and transcript may not be made available to anyone without my express permission until _____ after which it may be made available to general
date
research.

The parties hereto agree that the entire tape and transcript shall not be made available to anyone other than the parties hereto until _____except with the express
date

permission of _____ .
interviewee

Closed, Some Pages

The following transcript pages and the tape relating thereto shall be closed to all users until _____ except with the express permission of _____ . Transcript pages:
date   interviewee
_____ .

Limited Publication Rights Except With Permission

It is agreed the Library will not authorize publication of the transcript or *any substantial* part thereof during my lifetime without my permission, but the Library may authorize researchers and others to make brief quotations therefrom without my permission.

No Publication Without Permission

It is agreed the Library will not authorize publication by others of the transcript or *any* part thereof during my lifetime without my express permission.

Interviewee Retains Publication Rights

I reserve all literary property rights to the interview until _____, at which time these
date
literary property rights shall vest in The Regents of the University of California.

Fig. 20. Some restrictive clauses which can be added to the legal agreement.

10

Completing the Transcript

How you finish up the transcript will depend upon your goals. If local public relations are important to your continuation and funding, then a neatly typed, bound transcript with photographs and some illustrative materials will go a long way to sell your program. If widespread research use is the prime goal, then a well done subject-name index plus a cumulative index to your whole collection will be more important than the neat typing. Probably you will want to create both an attractive and usable manuscript.

However grandiose your goals, keep in mind that oral history transcripts are still research documents, not publications, and that it is unlikely you will be circulating more than ten copies. (Our very best seller, Dorothea Lange, "The Making of a Documentary Photographer" is in 26 libraries, and that is far below even the number of copies requested of a research paper someone may deliver at an academic conference.) So, without sanctioning slovenly workmanship, I suggest you don't aim for or claim perfection. Don't feel you must do five proofreadings to be sure you haven't let a typographical error slip by or scrambled a page number in the index. Try to provide a good basic research document with the emphasis on aids to its use.

Step one, when you get the transcript back, is to look it over carefully to find out if the narrator has cleared up all the questionable passages. It may be necessary to telephone or write again if something is still unclear. In making a change in a word, phrase, or tense, the narrator may inadvertently have changed the sentence from correct grammar to incorrect. That must be corrected to reflect the narrator's intent.

Whether to Final Type or Not

Again you must make a decision: whether to retype the corrected transcript, or to deposit it as is with corrections. Your decision should depend on the nature of your project, how important an attractive end product is, the size of your budget, and the expectations of your funding agency (or your expectations of getting funding if you can prove the worth of your project.)

If the interview is in the nature of an autobiographical memoir which the narrator wants on her family bookshelf, or if it is on a subject that will be widely used and perhaps copies requested by other historical agencies, or if the funding agency sees it in part as a recognition of achievement which will possibly go into the agency's library (memoirs of the leaders of our school, our church, our business, our profession,) then it should be retyped and an attractive and easily used manuscript prepared.

On the other hand, if the interview or series of interviews is primarily for limited research use, (perhaps that series of brief interviews on that disputed municipal election of 1964 and perhaps with many of the interviews under some sort of restricted use), it would not be worthwhile to retype, and researchers might prefer to work with a transcript that shows the corrections. Inexpensive photo copy methods now make it possible to give the narrator a copy of her corrected manuscript and to make copies for other libraries if that is desired. If you do not retype and the narrator has asked you to eliminate some pages or certain remarks, you may have to retype those pages as it would not be keeping your end of the bargain to leave what has been eliminated still visible in any way. Some offices only make available to researchers a xeroxed copy from which all deleted or under-seal-for-a-time passages have been blocked out by placing a paper over them before xeroxing.

Whether you retype or not, or indeed, if you simply deposit the tapes with a table of tape contents, certain bibliographic information is necessary. See the section on Front and Back Pages for these requirements.

Final Typing Procedures

1. Prepare the transcript for the final typist. Assuming that the editor has already checked the narrator's corrections to be sure they are clear, now give the transcript a last, fast run-through to be sure all spelling and style matters are consistent and that the headings and subheadings are marked in the proper places. If you have decided to use some illustrative materials with the transcript itself, or to refer to them, then footnotes may need to be added, and the placement of the illustrative material indicated so the typist can get the pagination right.

2. Early in the project, prepare a format sheet so the typist will know how to lay out the pages. The editor should go over the transcript with the typist to be sure matters as headings (a new page), subheadings (no new page), footnotes, etc. are clear. The typist should have a copy of the same style sheet the editor has used and should take some responsibility for catching things that are not consistent throughout, for example, capitalization of government agencies, how numbers are written. Unless the editor has gone over the transcript several times with a fine-tooth comb, some inconsistencies are bound to remain.

In our office, we have decided on a final typed format using single space, double-space between paragraphs and between speakers, and several lines between headings. We also use more paragraphs than absolutely necessary, because reading a long, single-spaced passage is hard. Single spacing allows one to get more on a page, and, while it may cut down on the number of completed transcript pages one can brag about at the end of the year, it also lessens the cost of producing extra copies (xerox cost per page) and the shelf space the library must allocate to the final transcripts.

As described in the Transcribing Format section, we prefer to use the name of the speaker rather than the initials; the name of the speaker appears at the top of the page even though the speech is a continuation from the previous page, and the speaker is named again after a subheading. Ease of reading within the context of fewer pages is the goal.

3. You will need two copies—the ribbon copy, and one copy for

proofreading, indexing, etc. This can be a carbon copy or a xerox of the ribbon copy. We have concluded a xerox of the ribbon copy is cheaper because that incorporates the correction of typing errors. If you use a carbon, the typist must correct the carbon also; otherwise the proofreader will mark for correction words that have already been corrected. In thinking about costs, labor is usually a more precious commodity than expenses such as xeroxing.

4. List the names of the transcriber, the final typist, and anyone else who did substantial work on the transcript. We list them at the end of the main body of the interview, right after "End of Interview" and before the index.

Figure 21 shows sample pages of final typed transcript.

Proofreading

Proofing the xerox or carbon copy of the final typed transcript can be done by one (or two) of the clerical workers, or by the interviewer-editor, or by the transcriber, but not by the final typist. I recommend that it be done by the interviewer-editor, who bears prime responsibility for the successful completion of the interview, as he is the person most likely to catch an unobvious error, for example, a paragraph omitted, or a "not" left out which totally changes the meaning. If proofing is done by someone previously unfamiliar with the interview, then you really need two persons, one to read the corrected transcript aloud, the other to check the copy.

The proofreader(s) should read through the proofing copy, marking corrections above the errors and in the right margin. While some projects require the use of standard proofreaders' symbols, we find that the majority of our staff are not familiar with those symbols and that they are not necessary.

Corrections can be made on the ribbon copy with correction fluid or correction tape immediately, or the proofing copy can next be used for preparing the index. Index items can be indicated in the left margin. In our office we find it easiest to prepare the index and the front and back pages before doing the corrections, and then to return the corrected, proofing copy to the final typist to do all the finishing work at one time.

Vaughan: afterwards became district attorney for Los Angeles County.

[End Side 1, Begin Side 2]
Money for College

Baum: Did most of your friends have to partially work their way through school, or at least not go to as expensive a school as Stanford?

Vaughan: Most of those I knew *did* work their way, in part at least, including myself.

Stoner [Reginald] didn't have to, but he did it. Omar Cavins* did it *all* himself. Forker [Wilfred] got help from his sister, Alma, who was teaching school in or near Bakersfield.

Earl Warren needed no help at all. His father was not a rich man. He was a carpenter. When times were dull and there were no jobs for him, he bought materials and *built* houses and rented them out. By the time Earl was in high school, his father was independent. I mean to say he had enough income coming in from property to support his family. He sometimes had plumbers do special work, but he himself was a carpenter and, for the most part built the houses himself. But Earl Warren did work at the end of his sophomore year, I am quite sure. He may have in his freshman year. I am almost sure that he did little or no work at the end of this third year.

Baum: Are you talking about college or high school?

Vaughan: High school. But what they were doing was getting money to go to college, you see.

Now Earl Warren, that summer, if he did any work it was in the early part of the summer, because I remember that about the middle of the summer, he came down here and spent some time in Long Beach; just taking it easy and having a good time at the beach.

He was able to do that, which a lot of us couldn't do. I was able to do it that summer because of special circumstances. Anyway, I remember seeing him down here. We went swimming together at the Long Beach plunge.

---

*See Cavins, Omar, "Coming of Age in Bakersfield," 1971, an interview in the Earl Warren Series.

Fig. 21. A final typed manuscript page.

Drinkers and Non-Drinkers

Baum: Was there any feeling of social distinction in your class, say, between Earl Warren, whose father was really just a mechanic, and your own type of persons, who were really more academic. . . .

Vaughan: No, no. There was a greater cleavage along another line. There was a lot of drinking in high school and I was a non-drinker. A total abstainer. That marked me as an outcast by certain groups. Some would tolerate me, and some of them liked me. I had friends there, yes. But during the first two years I was frequently reminded that I was a "baby, drinking milk," instead of a "man's drink," and all that sort of thing.

And of the boys that are here, [looking at senior class picture] I'm getting personal here, [little laugh] talking about people's habits.

Earl Warren—I don't think he drank much in high school. He certainly never got drunk. He may have taken an occasional drink. He was not a total abstainer. But he certainly didn't waste his energies on liquor.

Forker drank rather freely, but did not make a practice of getting drunk, although he *did* get drunk sometimes.

Omar Cavins was not a teetotaler, but he certainly drank very little himself and deplored heavy drinking by others.

Denton Stockton didn't drink at all.

Baum: And you were a teetotaler?

Vaughan: I was a teetotaler.

Baum: It still sounds like reasonable friends you could go around with. . . .

Vaughan: Oh, yes. I could be friends with them. But this is a select group. Mind you, the ones who were hard to contend with are not here. They didn't last to become seniors.

Young Romances

Baum: Did any romances come out of this, permanent romances, out of this class?

Fig. 21 (Continued).

Front and Back Pages

These constitute the bibliographic and use guides to the interview. They can be as basic or as elaborate as you can afford. The information to be included is listed below in descending order of indispensibility.

Essential Information for Cataloging and Bibliographic Retrieval (Library Use)

1. *Name of the narrator* (and somewhere there should be birth, and eventually, death dates if available).

2. *Major subject of interview*—this should be the title. Try for something more descriptive than "Recollections," "Onward and Upward," or "After Me Cometh a Builder" (one of ours, insisted upon by the memoirist). If your library does not have an elaborate subject cataloging system, this title may be the only aid the researcher has to finding the interview.

3. *Name of your project and institution.*

4. *Date.* This could be the date of the interview, or the date of completion—try to make it clear what date it is.

5. *Name of interviewer*—some projects tend to conceal the interviewer as just part of the team, and this may be appropriate if the interviewers work with a set questionnaire, but for individualized interviews, the interviewer should get the credit, or the blame, right there in the title pages.

6. *Conditions of use*—are there restrictions on use? Is it open for research, must permission be obtained for citing or quoting, and if so, from whom? Make sure that is right there so there will be no slip-up on meeting these conditions.

7. *Contents of the interview.* This may be a table of contents, keyed to the pages of the transcript, or it may be the table of tape contents, keyed to the tape by either time segments or footage indicator numbers. This is to show the user what subjects are discussed and about where he might find that subject if he is not interested in the whole.

For some short, one-topic interviews this may not be essential, the title representing the topic. The longer the interview, the more topics covered. The more likely the interview is to have value to a variety of users, the more important it is to have a detailed description of contents.

Essential Information for the User to Evaluate the Interview

8. *How did you come to have this interview* (called *provenance* in archivist language;) the Preface. This should be a description of the project and its responsibilities, and of the special subproject of which this is a part. The source of funding and other interviews in the same series should be indicated. The preface may describe briefly what the oral history process is. It should be signed by the project director and dated.

9. *The circumstances of the particular interview,* the Interview History. Here is the chance to give the dates of the interviews, and some account of how it went. Was the narrator eager to record, or only willing to give you a little time, did she check her own papers first or ask you to do so, did she edit heavily or not at all; did she give supporting papers and if so, what, and where are they. It is in the Interview History that the interviewer can say, very politely, something about the narrator as a person, give a glimpse of her home or office, family or work associates, or describe any physical problems that might have impeded the interview—illness, deafness, poor eyesight. The interviewer may provide some advice to the researcher on where to find other information on the narrator, other interviews that deal with the same topic, or books and papers that may contain corroborating or conflicting material. It should be signed by the person who wrote it (preferably the interviewer, possibly an editor) and dated.

10. *An Index to the Interview.* Even with a well done table of contents, an index is almost essential to retrieval of tidbits of information about persons, corporate entities, institutions, and subjects. A name-place index is very easy to do, a subject index is more difficult. If index entries are prepared on cards, it is only a small step further to file them cumulatively, thereby developing an index to all of your interviews which will very greatly increase the usability of the entire collection.

Helpful Additions for the User

11. *A vita of the narrator.* A chronological, factual listing of the narrator's passage through life, such as a *Who's Who* entry, will be a great help to the user in following the interview. If all of the narrator's life is not covered in the interview, such a vita will give some indication of what she was doing before and after the events of the interview, and her credentials for speaking.

12. *An introduction by a colleague of the narrator.* This is especially desirable in the use of a lengthy autobiographical memoir. Someone else in the narrator's field may be able to indicate the narrator's significance in the field. Or a colleague may be able to fill in personal characteristics or examples which do not come out in the narrator's first-person account but are essential to an understanding of how she functioned.

13. *Bibliography of writings* by the narrator, or list of the narrator's works.

14. *Information on the Interviewer.* This is not absolutely essential; still, the interviewer plays a very large part in the final result of the interview. The user will wish to know who this person is and what his background is. For further information about the narrator, perhaps for an introduction to her personally (if still alive), the user may wish to get in touch with the interviewer. If the interview was well researched, the interviewer will know a great deal about the subject and about other resources, not all of which will appear in the Interview History.

Samples of Front Pages

Figures 22-28 are some sample front pages: a title page, a table of contents, a legal agreement page, a preface, and an interview history. Because there are many other possible arrangements, I have also included a list of alternate statements gleaned from the front and back pages of other projects.

The most important back pages are the index, which will be discussed in the next section.

Oral History Committee
Central City Library Associates

Central City Public Library
Central City, California

Morris Kleiner
RECOLLECTIONS OF FAMILY, COMMUNITY, AND BUSINESS:
POLAND, CANADA, AND TACOMA, WASHINGTON, 1889-1974

An Interview Conducted by
Malca Chall in 1972

Fig. 22. A sample title page.

Memories
of
the Pajaro Valley

AN INTERVIEW WITH
EDWARD PORTER PFINGST

Edward Porter Pfingst was interviewed on January 21, 1972, at the Valley Convalescent Hospital in Watsonville, California. Hubert Wyckoff, President of the Pajaro Valley Historical Association, conducted the interview which was recorded and taped on a machine provided by the Friends of the Library, and operated by Mrs. Seely Sumpf, librarian of the Watsonville Public Library.

The tape is lodged at the Watsonville Public Library; and the interview has been reduced to narrative form and published by the Pajaro Valley Historical Association for sale at its museum as part of a series entitled, "Memories of the Pajaro Valley."

Done at Watsonville, California, September, 1973.

Fig. 23. A sample title page that very neatly incorporates all the essential bibliographical information.

TABLE OF CONTENTS—Morris Kleiner

Fig. 24. A sample table of contents. This contents is for an interview on family, the lumber business, and local history, and was carefully planned before taping. If sections were out of order, they were moved to the appropriate place before final typing. Copies of the transcript go to the family and to various historical libraries.

PREFACE

This manuscript is based on a tape-recorded interview conducted for the Center for History and Philosophy of Physics of the American Institute of Physics, the tape and the manuscript being the property of the Institute. I have read the transcript and have made only minor corrections and emendations. The reader is asked to bear in mind, therefore, that he is reading a transcript of the spoken, rather than the written, word.

The manuscript may be read, quoted from and cited for purposes of research only by scholars approved by the Institute at such place as is made available for purposes of research by the Institute. No reproduction of the manuscript, either in whole or in part, may be made by microphoto, typewriter, photostat, or any other means, except with the written permission of the Institute in which permission, if given during my lifetime, I must join.

(signed)_____

(date)   _____

AIP OH-1

Fig. 25. A sample legal agreement page used by Center for History and Philosophy of Physics, American Institute of Physics.

This manuscript is open for research purposes. All literary rights in the manuscript, including the right to publish, are reserved to The Bancroft Library of the University of California at Berkeley. No part of the manuscript may be quoted for publication without the written permission of the Director of The Bancroft Library of the University of California at Berkeley.

Requests for permission to quote for publication should be addressed to the Regional Oral History Office, 486 Library, and should include identification of the specific passages to be quoted, anticipated use of the passages, and identification of the user.

Fig. 26. One form of preface including permission to quote information.

PREFACE

San Francisco Bay Maritime History Series

The following interview is one of a series of tape-recorded recollections devoted to the history of San Francisco Bay in the first half of the twentieth century. This was an especially colorful, active period of momentous technological and sociological change in American maritime affairs, and San Francisco Bay reflected the period well. For the economic historian, the reminiscences illustrate the changes in San Francisco Bay that took place in response to worldwide maritime conditions and to changes in California; for the maritime buff, they are full of the bustle, color and variegated characters of a lively shipping port serving deep-water, coastwise, and river and bay traffic.

Thanks are extended to the Crowley Launch and Tug Company for permission to research in their extensive scrapbook collection and for the help and advice given by members of the firm over the years that the series has been in progress. Our gratitude also to the staff of the San Francisco Maritime Museum for the use of their historical documentation and for their help in checking out names, dates, and facts.

The Regional Oral History Office was established to tape record autobiographical interviews with persons prominent in the history of California and the West. The Office is under the administrative supervision of James D. Hart, director of The Bancroft Library.

Willa K. Baum
Department Head
Regional Oral History Office

11 September 1971
Regional Oral History Office
486 The Bancroft Library
University of California at Berkeley

Fig. 27. A sample preface which includes information about the interview.

Interview History

Francis E. Vaughan was a classmate of Earl Warren's at Bakersfield High School, class of 1908, and at the University of California at Berkeley, class of 1912. He was interviewed by the Regional Oral History Office as a part of the Earl Warren Oral History Project in order to document the life of students in those two schools.

Interviewer: Willa K. Baum, director, Regional Oral History Office.

Conduct of the
Interview: A single interview was held on January 13, 1970, at Dr. Vaughan's spacious home in Pasadena. Although still active as president of VEMCO, a drafting equipment firm he founded after leaving his position as geologist for Shell Oil Company in 1938, he had taken the day off to reminisce about his school days for the tape recorder. The only interruptions were several telephone calls from the burglar alarm company, just checking the equipment, and a brief coffee break midway in the interview. Dr. Vaughan had several mementos of the class of 1908 that brought back memories, as did the photo of the class.

Editing: The typed transcript was sent to Dr. Vaughan, who asked for some time to "go over the transcript with reasonable care and attempt to effect some improvements, . . . The most glaring faults relate to disorderly use of language. . . ."

                Two months later the transcript was returned, neatly retyped as corrected, with a covering letter admitting to striking out repetitious phrases, simple improvements in wording and punctuation, but the relief that, "Despite my numerous changes, I am sure that there remain sufficient points of awkwardness, perhaps some real faults, to avoid the 'stiffness of perfection'."

Willa K. Baum, Director
Regional Oral History Office

24 May 1971
486 The Bancroft Library
University of California at Berkeley

Fig. 28. An interview history.

Photographs and Illustrative Materials

One or more photographs will be well worth the cost. How much more lively a written transcript and tape become when you have before you a photograph of the speaker. And the photograph(s) can be used if the tape is ever made into a slide-tape show.

Try to borrow or take a photo (if you have any skills with the camera) of your narrator at her present age; also borrow one showing the narrator and colleagues in the period discussed in the interview. We find it saves work to prepare a typed caption for the photograph, then have the photograph and the caption copied onto another negative, and then return the original to the narrator.

Other illustrative materials that are easily and cheaply xeroxed and add much interest could be a crucial letter or telegram, a newspaper clipping, a political campaign letter with the letterhead showing the names of endorsers, maps, etc. These are more effective placed in the transcript at the places where they are discussed than lumped together in an appendix.

How Many Copies to Prepare

If possible, try to estimate how many copies you will need and have them duplicated and bound all at once. You will need a complimentary copy for the narrator, one for the depository, and one for your own office (if you are not the depository). This is in addition to the ribbon copy which should be held unbound and unused so that it can always be copied on request.

You may wish to prepare a copy for a central depository, perhaps the state historical society or the state library. More than likely, your narrator will request extra copies *after* she has received the complimentary copy, and you will have to go through the whole duplication, assembling, binding process again.

Binding

I cannot insist too strongly on the importance of binding the finished transcript. In the early days of oral history, transcripts were often stored loose in boxes, or punched and put into ring binders. Not only did this allow for pages to be lost or scrambled, but it negated the whole effect of the effort that had gone into the interviews. Of all the investments you make in oral history, a modest binding will be your best return for your money in terms of public relations and security of the transcript.

Many libraries have ways to bind pamphlets or periodicals, and they can bind the transcripts in the same way. Libraries are also usually very slow; your narrator may die waiting for her copy. Duplicating services often can provide spiral bindings with heavy paper covers that may suffice, although it will not be adequate for heavy library use. Velo-bind is an instant hardcover binding, with lettering, and is available at many duplicating services at around $5 a copy. For short interviews you can even use cardboard binders with fasteners (Acco Press binders).

11

Indexing

An index will greatly increase the usefulness of the transcript. It is not as essential as a table of contents, based on descriptive headings and subheadings in the body of the transcript, which may be enough for some short interviews. But for an interview which deals with specific historical events, persons who played a role in the region's history, or matters about which the project is gathering information from a variety of narrators, an index becomes the key to wide usage. This is particularly true if the index entries to each transcript are then filed together to form a cumulative index to your whole collection.

An index can serve an editorial purpose also. By making accessible information on a topic which may be scattered throughout the interview, it will save the editor having to cut and paste to bring the material together in the text of the interview. The final transcript can therefore remain closer to the tape without losing usability.

A Simple Name Index or a Subject Index

Again a decision, whether to prepare a simple name index or a subject index. By subject index, I mean a dictionary-type index which lists names, titles, and subjects in alphabetical sequence. A subject index will be more valuable but difficult; a simple name index will be less valuable but easy.

Anyone on the program staff can prepare a name index; that is, read through the transcript; underline the names of persons, institutions, businesses, government agencies, towns; write them down on cards with page numbers; alphabetize them; and type up the list. In some instances, although a name is mentioned, there will be no information about that entity that anyone would want to know.

Considering the ease of doing a name index, it is the bare minimum for a properly done transcript. And even a name index will markedly increase the accessibility of information in the transcript.

On the other hand, a subject index involves much time, thought, and discrimination. It requires knowing where the collection will eventually go for deposit and how it will fit into that library's collection, keeping abreast of current trends in research and what the vocabularies for those subjects are, and making an educated guess as to who the users of the collection may be and what information they may be seeking. All of that effort will be worth it if broad usage is your goal and your interviews are good.

Again, as in previous decisions, you will have to weigh the significance of your interviews against the limitations of your budget and staff time. My recommendation is to do a subject index if you want your interviews to get any more than purely local use, and to do a cumulative index to your collection.

Indexing Principles For an Oral History Collection

What to Index

In deciding what to index, consider what your areas of emphasis are as well as who your likely patrons will be. You had to consider this in planning who to interview and what questions to ask so it is not new ground. Index heavily the subjects you emphasize because users will come to your collection to find those subjects. Index lightly the many odds and ends of information that will show up in the collection.

For example, our own program is basically about California and we would index any town or region in California about which there is substantive information. But one of our narrators described his work in China: the towns, the government officials, schools, customs, etc. We have simply lumped those under "China", with a few subheadings. If we were doing a series of interviews on Chinese history, the index on that chapter would be much more detailed. Conversely, our office is doing a history of the California wine industry. In those transcripts we have separate detailed indexes for named wines and varieties of grapes because we know the many writers on wine connoisseurship will be looking for those references.

If your area of emphasis is local history, your material will be used to prepare booklets on historic sites, newspaper articles on anniversaries of local events, biographical accounts of leading citizens or local characters. Index those topics heavily.

Do Not Underindex or Overindex

Underindexing may be a budget problem, for which you can be excused. But overindexing is a waste of staff time and ultimately a waste of the user's time and that is inexcusable. Overindexing is the result of not thinking about the uses of the collection, but rather of turning loose on the collection someone who has had a brief course in indexing, who writes down every name and possible subject, and cross-references everything. Results: a large, beautiful, expensive index which will cause the researcher to chase a dozen nonproductive leads for every productive one—a problem serious enough to cause the Committee on Oral History of the Society of American Archivists to put on the agenda of a recent meeting, "how to prevent overindexing of oral history."

As Martha T. Wheeler put it, in her restrained way, in *Indexing, Principles Rules & Examples,* "It is *unworkmanlike* to inflate the index until it rivals the text in bulk."

Included in the samples is an overindexed index.

Do Not Index Noninformation

Many mentions of a name or subject are of no information and to index them is just to annoy the researcher. "Yes, I opened my office in 1922—I remember T. Edwards had just been elected mayor the day I hung out my shingle." The eager indexer puts, "Edwards, Mayor T., 18" into the transcript index, and from there it enters the cumulative index. The researcher on "powers of the mayor's office" or "T. Edwards" or "local government" finds the reference, gets out the interview, turns to page 18, and finds that T. Edwards was elected mayor, which any town history can tell him with considerably more authority.

Users want to find real information, maybe new or maybe corroborating what they have found in other references, or they want to find some very quotable quotes from an eyewitness to liven up their writings or audio presentations.

Selecting Subject Headings

Select the subject headings that most adequately describe the subject, and which you think the users will try to find. This, like selecting who and what to interview about is a little like trying to outguess the future. Do the best you can. In a college history series, perhaps headings like "Wonder team", "Berkeley fire", "Illustrious Class of 1912" are what your users will look for so use them. You can always cross-reference from more scholarly headings; i.e. athletics, 13–15. *See also* Wonder team.

If your collection is sociological, perhaps a study of the assimilation of an ethnic group into the community, your subject headings may be more on the order of "child-rearing patterns", "sex roles in the family", "marriage customs." You will find guidance for subject headings in the indexes of books on immigration or cultural anthropology. Keep in mind that your users may be academics from afar as well as the local preservers of the ethnic group's traditions.

A local history collection should index buildings, streets, events—for us "Earthquake & Fire, 1906" is always an index item because it is a heavy topic of research. If your collection is going to a library that has a local history collection of books, newspapers, memorabilia, try to coordinate your subject headings with those the library is already using. Work with the local librarian on this.

The appropriate vocabulary for subject headings changes with the times, sometimes so rapidly as to make an indexer's head swim. Do not despair if within a few years many of your subject words have changed. If your heading "Unemployment, California State Department of" has to become "Employment, California State Department of," and five years later, "Manpower Resources Development, California State Department of," just go on with the new heading and refer the user backward and forward with a *See also* reference.

Choose headings that are appropriate to the period you are

documenting. For example, although we were tape-recording in the 1970s, our program settled on "Negroes" as a heading because we were documenting Negro political leaders of the 1930s and 1940s and that was the historically appropriate term as well as being the term that was acceptable to our narrators. As we begin to document the 1960s, we will shift to "blacks" with a "*See also* Negroes" cross reference to lead users to the earlier material.

There are subject heading books which librarians use for cataloging and it would be worth your while to refer to them before choosing general subject headings. Of these, I recommend you buy either *Sears List of Subject Headings* ($12) or *Cross-Reference Index, A Subject Heading Guide* ($22.50) for the office. The *Sears List* has an excellent introduction on how to select subject headings which should be read by your indexers, and the editors have thoughtfully provided very wide margins to the subject headings so you can pencil in subject headings which you have selected for your own collection. *Cross-Reference Index* uses somewhat more up-to-date headings than *Sears* because it draws its headings from periodical indexes as well as the Library of Congress subject lists. Most libraries have the *Reader's Guide to Periodical Literature;* use the latest full year guide to check contemporary subjects (the monthly cumulative guides are too brief to cover all subjects). The *New York Times Index* is also an excellent guide to current usage.

A Master Subject Heading List

Once you have thoughtfully selected the heading for a subject, stick to it. If you keep changing your subject headings, your cumulative index will either be cluttered with cross-reference cards or your users will miss half of the references. To enable the indexers to use the same headings, set up a master subject heading list. This can be a card file, or for easier use, a typed list which you update from time to time.

As an example, in our interviews we have many references to campaigns and legislation for fair housing, fair employment, equal accommodations, etc. There were many headings they could have been indexed under: racial segregation, racial desegregation, discrimination, Proposition 14 (a fair housing initiative); the proper terminology changes daily. We finally decided to list all these items under "civil rights" with subentries. The master subject heading list reads "Civil Rights—includes housing, employment, accommodations, education, etc."

You may do interviews in different series, and the topics may be different enough to warrant separate master subject heading lists. If you have a teacher's strike series, a great flood series, a cattle industry series, and a uranium mining series, you will surely need specialized lists.

Included in the Samples is a master subject heading list (partial) for a Forest Service and forest industry series.

A Cumulative Index

A cumulative index is an invaluable guide to your whole collection. It is a card index, prepared by simply adding the individual interview index cards to a large alphabetical card file. Each card, which will already contain the heading and page numbers, just needs to have written or stamped on it the name of the narrator. Use the narrator's full name, you can soon get several interviews by persons with the same surname so don't abbreviate.

The cumulative index does add a modest additional task to the indexing, and that is to prepare a subject card for the major subjects of the interview. Let's say the entire John Smith interview deals with banking in Willows, California, a small agricultural town. Neither "banking" nor "Willows" need appear in the interview index because it is *all* about banking and Willows. But you will need to prepare subject entry cards for "banking" and "Willows" for the cumulative index, and refer the user to the John Smith interview, no pagination.

Let's say also that the table of contents reads "Starting Out as an Insurance Adjuster, 1902," and the chapter tells a bit about what an insurance adjuster did. No need to index that in the interview index since we can assume the user is able to read the table of contents as well as the index. But you will want to prepare a card for the cumulative index that reads, "Insurance adjusting, 1902. John Smith interview, pages 18–22."

Advice to Indexers

The following advice to indexers assumes you are preparing a subject index. It is also based on several premises which are a little different than those of most how-to-index manuals. First, it assumes that staff time for indexing is very limited, and that every step must be streamlined (even if it does leave room for error); two, that this is still a manuscript, not a published book, and does not warrant the endless checking and backchecking necessary for a book index. It assumes, third, that your users will be bright, if in a hurry, so if you can help them locate the material, they do not need any further coddling; and fourth, that you will file the individual transcript index cards in a cumulative index to the entire collection. With these premises in mind, you are ready to begin.

1. *Mark the proofing copy* (a xerox or carbon of the final typed transcript). It may already have been proofread and errors marked; or the indexer's first run-through may be used for proofing. In any event, errors should be noted on the (ample) right margin, index information on the (ample) left margin.

2. *Names.* Underline all proper names that should be indexed. These may be persons, places, companies, institutions, almost anything that gets a capital letter. Not all names should be indexed. For example, if it says "I was born the same year as King George V" or "I passed the Mercantile Building every day on my way to work," no researcher will thank you for indexing George V or the Mercantile Building. (This is a problem with computerized key-word-in-context indexing, too many wild goose chases.)

But whether a bit of information about someone is important or not may not be such an easy decision. For example, whether to include a listing of persons who attended a certain meeting, some of whom may never appear again in the transcript. This information may be well-documented otherwise, or more likely, be of no significance, but it just may be the missing clue to why one of those participants later did something else that was important. Mark the underlined names with a question mark and leave the decision to the interviewer who has done the background research on the subject. But don't spend too much time; it is cheaper to put in a doubtful entry than to investigate it fully.

3. *Subject Headings.* In the left margin, jot down tentative subject headings that come to mind as you read. On the next round, reconsider the phrases you have used. Is it one users will look for? Check the master subject heading list to see if there is not a heading already selected that would be more appropriate. If it is a new subject heading, and you are dubious about it, check the index of a published book on the subject. Check the *Sears List of Subject Headings* or *Cross-Reference Index;* maybe you will find a better heading, but probably not. Use published book indexes to give you ideas but don't feel constrained to follow someone else's lead. You are doing original research and there may be no accepted vocabulary that exactly covers your material.

Mark questionable headings for conference with the interviewer and other members of the program staff.

4. *Subentries.* Use subentries if you will have a great many entries under that heading. For example, our office has 150 interviews on Governor Earl Warren's administration in California, each of which refers to Earl Warren in one context or another. It is necessary to add subentries to the heading "Earl Warren," and those can be arranged chronologically.

Warren, Governor Earl

      boyhood,   12
      as governor,   46
      attitude toward child care centers,   57–58
      attitude toward FEPC legislation,   96–97, 108

                                              TAREA PITTMAN

On the other hand, it is unnecessary coddling to use subentries for a person who only appears occasionally in the interviews. Let the user look for himself to see what it is about.

5. *Page entries.* If the discussion goes on for some pages more or less on the subject of the entry, use all the inclusive pages. For example, "Election, of 1936, 20–30," is easier than "Election of 1936, 20–22, 24–25, 27–30." The user will have to read the whole section anyhow to understand the context. Oral history is not like an almanac, packed full of discrete facts. It requires some reading around the subject to understand what is being said. Neither do you have to do all the work for the user.

6. *Compile entries.* Write entries on a 3 x 5 card or onto a sheet of paper marked off in alphabetical divisions, whichever is easier for you to handle. We find that for short indexes, sheets of paper are easier to handle; you can more quickly run down the C listing and spot whether you have an entry for "CCC (Civilian Conservation Corps)" and just add another page number than shuffle through all your C cards. You will still have to prepare cards for the final alphabetization and then to file in the cumulative index.

But even if you use cards to begin with, do not follow the recommendation given in every indexing book that you prepare a separate card for every time a subject entry is mentioned—i.e. if Smith, John D. is liberally sprinkled throughout the transcript, you are advised to prepare 30 separate cards for Smith, John D., each with one page listed on it. That sort of painstaking work is only for a published book where it is essential you do not make an error in the index.

7. *Prepare Index Cards.* Type index cards (or hand write them neatly). These cards are for the interview index and the cumulative index. Leave several empty lines at the top so you can later change the subject heading without retyping the card. You may use one heading in the interview index, a more inclusive one in the cumulative index. In a College History Series interview with the dean of students on student housing, the main heading may be "Chancellor's Office." In the cumulative index, it will become "Central City College" and "Chancellor's Office" will be a subentry.

Your blank lines may permit you to change the heading as the years change the vocabulary. Your "Mexican-Americans" cards can be changed to "Chicanos" and some years later to whatever heading is being used.

```
+------------------------------+   +------------------------------+
| Central City College         |   | Chicanos                     |
|     Chancellor's Office, 15–19|  |   Mexican Americans          |
|                              |   |     agricultural labor, 44–50|
|                              |   |                              |
|       ETHEL MOORE            |   |      NELSON EVEREST          |
+------------------------------+   +------------------------------+
```

8. *Whether to Index Front and Back Pages.* Ordinarily introductory and illustrative materials, appendices, and footnotes are not indexed. They are often items that are so full of references that you will breathe a sigh of relief to know you are not expected to index them. However, some of the illustrative materials you collect will be of such rare value that you will want to make sure users find them. Go ahead and index them. You do not have to abide by any indexing rules for oral history. Index what you think is important, fully or just partially; don't index what isn't.

9. *Cross References.* In the same way that an index allows you to leave information in the transcript just where it came to the narrator's mind without losing accessibility, so cross references allow you to go ahead indexing without having to come up with the final and definitive subject headings. Use *See* when you wish to refer the user to another wording, i.e. blind; programs for the. *See* Aid to the Blind, 14–18, 25–35, 77, 176–180. Use *See also* when there are related subjects, i.e. American Red Cross, 128, 132. *See also* Junior Red Cross.

A *See* reference means the user has to go to another item. Don't waste the user's time at no advantage to your program's typing time or page space. If there are not many page entries, it is just as easy to type an entry twice, with pages, as to use a *See*, i.e. "Twain, Mark (Samuel L. Clemens), 14" and also "Clemens, Samuel L. (Mark Twain), 14" is just as easy and less irritating than "Twain, Mark. *See* Samuel L. Clemens" plus "Clemens, Samuel L. (Mark Twain), 14. This would not be true if there were a number of page entries or subentries.

Final Typing the Index

1. Always put the name of the narrator on the index to prevent binding the wrong index in a transcript.

2. Leave several lines space between alphabetical divisions. If you later find you left out an entry, you have a little leeway within the alphabetical division to add without retyping the whole page. Typing indexes is slower going than narrative pages.

3. Names. Try to add the first name even if it isn't mentioned in the text, but don't spend a lot of time looking for it. And don't add it if you are not absolutely sure you have the right one.

If there are two persons of the same name, try to add some identification.

Johnson, Adam (1890–1960)   Jones, Robert (engineer)
Johnson, Adam (b. 1930)   Jones, Robert (teacher)

4. Format. Choose your own from any book you like. Rather than discuss punctuation, spacing, and other index questions, refer to the Sample Index that follows.

Proofing the Index

This will require two persons, one to read the index cards, the other to check if pagination is typed correctly. Try to have someone who is very familiar with the subject of the interview hold the copy. It is surprising how many errors in spelling names can get through as far as the index where they are finally caught by a knowledgeable person.

Filing the Cumulative Index Cards

You may wish to add and subtract some of the interview index cards before filing in the cumulative index. Add broad references to the whole interview, or sections that are identified by the table of contents in the interview and therefore are not in the interview index. For example, add a card on "Mining—John Smith" if the whole Smith interview deals with mining and therefore mining has not been a subject heading in the interview index. Once the user gets to the interview, he can use the table of contents, but the cumulative index is to get him to the interview.

Subtract entries that won't be sought in the cumulative index but do belong in the interview index. For example, an interview with Valeska Bary covers in some detail the Bary ancestors of New England and Illinois. In the interview index, they are all listed, because a copy of the interview may be sent to the Illinois Historical Society and because members of the family will want one. But for the cumulative index, "Bary family, 1–20," is sufficient.

An Easy Way Out—A Form Index

The high number of oral history programs that complain that they are backlogged on indexing their interviews, either in tape or in transcript, indicates that indexing is both difficult and less alluring than the actual interviewing. The backlog most often accumulates when there is a flood of interviews in a short time, and this most often occurs under the impetus of a special project: an institutional anniversary that will be celebrated by an interview series on its history; a class project on women in politics; an effort to preserve the history of an ethnic neighborhood that is about to be eradicated through urban development. In these special projects, a team of interviewers often goes out armed with a set of questions, and each interviewer may cover pretty much the same basic ground, as well as some individualized questions for each narrator.

The focus of the project and the questions to be asked can provide the subject headings for the index in advance. A master subject heading list can be set up that will make the indexing of the tapes or transcripts almost automatic.

Even quicker than indexing from an established subject list is to print up index forms for the special project, listing the subject headings in alphabetical order. We all know how much easier it is to fill in a form for even such routine information as one's name and address than to start from scratch to tell who one is. The printed index form can list the subject headings, with some space at the end of each alphabetical section for other names and subjects that are discussed in the interview.

All the indexer (who should be the interviewer) has to do is go through the interview, either listening to the tape or reading the transcript, and mark down the counter numbers or the page numbers when one of the listed subjects is mentioned. He will also have to write in unlisted names or subjects. Naturally, there will be no entries at all after some of the subject headings, and the write-in headings will be a bit out of alphabetical order, but the project will end up with all the interviews indexed in accessible fashion and the index items will be comparable from one interview to another. A form index is included in the samples.

Style Books and Indexing Aids

A Manual of Style. University of Chicago Press, Twelfth Edition, 1969, 546 pages. This style book has become the Bible of most publishers and journals. It covers everything you need to know, including indexing. The twelfth edition has gone so far in the direction of eliminating punctuation and lower-casing titles (the president of the United States) that a project dealing with old-timers may have to modify some of the rules. Nonetheless, this is *the* basic stylebook to begin with in preparing your own style sheet.

Words Into Type. Marjorie E. Skillin, Third Edition, 1974. Prentice-Hall, Englewood Cliffs, New Jersey, 583 pages. A substantial style book that will cover everything you need to know, and a good bit more, about typing manuscripts and then preparing them for publication. Highly recommended.

20,000 Words. Louis A. Leslie, 1959. McGraw-Hill Book Company, New York, 250 pages. This little handbook is primarily to help typists quickly in spelling and dividing words correctly. The brief section on "Punctuation Simplified" is excellent.

Indexing Your Book, A Practical Guide to Authors. Sina Spiker, 1963. University of Wisconsin Press, Madison. A very useful 28-page paperback. Do purchase.

Chatters: I prepared an itinerary for an all-day trip and it was handed over to one of the girls to tape, with copies for his office, campaign headquarters, etc., so he could be reached at any time.

type .
campaign

Fry: Warren was to speak there that night?

Chatters: Yes. When we came to the last item, which was Quincy, I had noted the town, the time, our first contact "Pop" Small the publisher, the dinner hour, banquet chairman, etc. The typed sheet given me to turn over to Warren read something like this:

campaigns

     4:00 P.M., Quincy, population small, etc., etc.

When Warren told them at the dinner how his schedule read he got one of the biggest laughs of the campaign, for the townspeople all knew that "Pop" with his five or six children was doing his best in the opposite direction. I remember we met publisher Small in his office earlier that afternoon. He was standing at a job press feeding some kind of election poster, at the same time attired in the usual ink-covered printer's apron.

Small,
Merrell F.
"Pop"

attired .

Friends will recall that M.F. (Pop) Small later served on Governor Warren's staff at the capitol, for some time as Departmental Secretary. Later he became U.S. Senator Tom Kuchel's administrative aid in Washington. A mutual agreement.

Kuchel,
Senator
Thomas

department.
secretary
aide

Comments on Warren as Governor, and the Warren Family

Fry: Was Mrs. Waren willing to take the peace and quiet of home?

Warren,
Nina (Mrs. Earl)

Warren

Chatters: Probably, I am not competent to answer; but an observation or too: I saw and heard enough to know she was a marvelous lady, certainly a wonderful mother and gracious person for the Mansion. I understand she had a new kitchen put in and made the old structure a real home for the eight of them.

two

Warren family

This may be getting ahead of my story, but after Warren became governor and one of his drivers at the Mansion took the children to school, they insisted on being let out a block or so away rather than be conspicuously chauffeured to the school by a guard.

Fig. 29. Sample of a final transcript, marked for errors and index entries.

MASTER SUBJECT HEADING LIST (Partial)

Forest Service & Forest Industries Series

Agriculture Adjustment Administration (AAA)
Agriculture, Department of
  Administration
  Secretary, powers of
  White House relations
Agriculture Yearbook
Alabama
Alaska (Region 10, USFS)
American Forest Products Association
American Forestry Association
Anderson-Mansfield Reforestation & Re-vegetation Act, 1949
Arkansas
Arizona
Associated Farmers
Bureau, Internal Revenue
  Business & Industrial Research Division
Bureau, Land Management
Bureau, Outdoor Recreation
Bureau, Public Roads
California (Region 5, USFS)
Capital factor in forest taxation
Capper Report

Civilian Conservation Corps (CCC)
Claims
Clarke-McNary Act
Colorado
Community Development
Congress, U.S.
Connecticut
Conservation organizations as a whole
Copeland Report
County government
Cruising
Delaware
Differential Timber Tax
Disaster Loan Corporation
Disease
  Timber
Eastern Pine Sales Corporation
Education
  Conservation education (teaching pro-grams)
  Professional schools
    Accreditation
    Technical training
  Schooling of [specific foresters names]

Fig. 30. A master subject heading list.

MASTER SUBJECT HEADINGS LIST

Use these key words only:

1. Acculturation	13. Fishing	25. Plantation
2. Business	14. Food	26. Politics
3. Communication	15. Health/Welfare	27. Recreation
4. Community	16. Housing	28. Religion
5. Crime	17. Immigration/Emigration	29. Statehood
6. Customs	18. Job	30. Strikes
7. Death	19. Leadership	31. Transportation
8. Depression	20. Marriage/Dating	32. Union
9. Education	21. Mechanization	33. Wages
10. Ethnicity	22. Miscellaneous	34. War
11. Family	23. Organizations	35. Working Conditions
12. Farming	24. Paternalism	

After the key word, add brief, explanatory names, phrases, and/or dates if pertinent.

Fig. 31. Master subject headings list from the Ethnic Studies Oral History Project, University of Hawaii at Manoa. The project studies the Waialua/ Haleiwa community as an example of plantation and small towns in Hawaii.

INDEX

Fig. 32. An example of bad indexing. It is overindexed, the choice of headings is poor. The index is far too long for a six-page transcript.

INDEX—John Doe

AAA (Agricultural Adjustment Administration),   44, 78–80
Agriculture:
  Acreage limitation,   79–89
  County and state fairs,   36–39
  Irrigation for,   79–82
  Lobbying by,   80–89
Albany, California,   11–14, 21–34

Becker, Mrs. John (Eva Jones),   14
Bernstorff, Count Johann von,   27
Birth control,   31–33
Blacks. *See* Negroes
Brendon, _____,   7
Brobeck, Phleger & Harrison (attorneys),   180
Brown, Governor Edmund G., appointments,   71–73
Budget, state,   106–107, 115–116
Burton, Mrs. Richard (Elizabeth Taylor),   102, 105

California State:
  Allocation Board,   66–68, 71
  Department of Corrections,   53
  Department of Finance,   31, 34, 94–97
  Department of Social Welfare,   127–128
  Water Resources Board,   83
Canned food:
  Dog food,   116–118
  Fish processing,   108–115, 121
  Olives,   118–119, 121
  Spinach processing,   107, 118
  Tomatoes,   276–277
Cannery Act, 1925,   119–120
Chamber of Commerce,   45–46
Chicanos. *See* Mexican Americans
Christian Science Monitor,   88
Church of Jesus Christ of Latter Day Saints (Mormon Church),   32–40
Civil rights:
  FEPC legislation,   88–93, 101–102, 117
  Fair housing,   125
  Nevada public accommodations law,   140–141
  See also Proposition   14
Clemens, Samuel L. (Mark Twain),   41–47
Community Chest,   120–125
Conscription:
  World War II,   18–20
  Korean War,   36–37
  Vietnam War,   73–75

Fig. 33. A good index, illustrating format and some of the types of entries.

Fig. 33 (Continued).

Fig. 33 (Continued).

INDEX: Women in Politics
Interview with *Ann Ellison, City Council-
woman, Central City*

A
Attitudes:
    men towards women, *10, 15*
    women towards women, *3*
    women towards men, *5, 14*
    general towards women, *3, 8, 14, 15*
American Hospitals Association, 3

B
Background, personal, *1*
Bussing, 20–22

C
Campaigning, *2, 36*
Chisolm, Shirley,
Colleagues, relation with, *1, 3, 4*
Constituents, reaction to, *15*
Criticism, reaction to, *8, 17*
Candidates, hostility, 4
City clerk, 7

D
Decision to be a candidate, *6*
Decision to take appointed position,
Decision making process, *12*

E
Effectiveness, *8, 22*
Elective offices held, *4*
Evaluating the experience,
Education, 9

F
Family, *6, 27*
    budgeting time, 18
    husband, 7
Financing campaign, 4–6

G

H
Higher office, plans for, *22*
Homework, 4

I
Independence, *6*
Information, sources of,
Initiative,
Issues, *5*

J
Judges, endorsement of, 6
Judson, Chas. A., campaign aide, 283

K

L
League of Women Voters, 9
Los Angeles Times, 17

M
Mayors, 12
Men:
    reaction to criticism,
Miller, John J., 3, 4, 6, 13

N
News media, *5, 17*

O
*Ophals, Mary, administrative assis-
    tant, 8*

P
Prejudice, 18
PTA, 7
Q

R
Race,
Responsiveness, *13, 17*
Republican Woman's Club, 10

*Fig. 34. A form index. The subject headings were based on topics in the
questionnaire. Subject headings were already printed. Indexer adds page
numbers and additional headings.*

Indexing; Principles Rules & Examples. Martha T. Wheeler, 1957. New York State Library, University of the State of New York, Albany, 78 pages, paperback. First published in 1905, this is a practical guide to indexing. Out of print, try to use in the library.

Indexes & Indexing. Robert L. Collison, 1959. John de Graff, Inc., New York, 200 pages. A British book, probably too formal for oral history, but consult it if you need help in indexing.

Sears List of Subject Headings. Barbara M. Westby, editor, Tenth Edition, 1972. H. W. Wilson Company, New York, 570 pages. This has an excellent introduction on how to select subject headings. Wide margins allow you to pencil in new headings you can use for your collection. Recommended for purchase by oral history office.

Cross-Reference Index, A Subject Heading Guide. Thomas V. Atkins, editor, 1974. R. R. Bowker Company, New York, 255 pages. An easily used and applicable to oral history subject heading book. It won't answer all your questions. It includes entries from Library of Congress, Sears, Readers' Guide to Periodical Literature, New York Times Index, Public Affairs Information Service and Business Periodical Index, which results in more contemporary entries than Sears or Library of Congress lists.

Readers' Guide to Periodical Literature. Most libraries have this large cumulative, up-to-date set. Use it in the library to check out your prospective subject headings. Even more current in choice of vocabulary is the *New York Times Index*. If that set is available in your library, use it to check subject headings.

12

Depositing the Interview

The Choice of an Appropriate Depository

Probably you will have already selected the depository where your oral history materials will reside in perpetuity. Such a depository should have the following qualifications:

1. A permanent legal existence with a director to whom ownership and administration of the oral history materials can be assigned; for example, the Librarian of Central City Public Library.

2. A permanent building or space where the materials will be kept.

3. A regular staff that is prepared to handle special noncirculating materials; for example, supervision of the use of tape players by patrons, and carrying out of any restrictions such as getting permission to quote.

4. Regular hours when the depository is open and users can have access to the materials. (Not a historical society museum which is open from 2–4 p.m. on Thursdays only.)

5. Preferably located near the scene of the events covered in the oral history collection. Oral history materials should get civic and school use as well as academic research use. If you want to broaden the academic use, deposit another set of the finished transcripts in a central location, but keep the bulk of the materials in your home locality.

A Checklist of Items to Deposit

Try to have everything relating to one interview, or a series of interviews on a special topic, ready to deposit at one time. It is very hard for librarians to catalog materials properly if additional items keep dribbling in. For each interview, have the following items ready when you deposit it:

1. Tape(s), properly labeled on the tape box and the reel or cassette. If the narrator requested deletion of subject matter, those passages should have been erased.

2. A Table of Tape Contents, and maybe the notes the interviewer took during the interview if they include more guidance to the tape than is in the table of tape contents and/or the transcript.

3. The transcript, if any, in whatever is the most completed stage you brought it to, with photographs and illustrative material.

4. Legal agreement.

5. Supporting materials, additional photographs, papers, and other relevant memorabilia.

A Ceremonial Presentation to the Narrator

One of the most gratifying bonus values of oral history is the implicit recognition it gives the narrator that her life has had some significance that is worth documenting. The narrator has probably enjoyed the oral history process, but she has also dedicated a varying, often substantial, amount of time and thought to the production of a valuable interview. It is only appropriate, and socially useful, that the narrator be properly and publicly thanked.

At the minimum, this should involve a well worded thank-you letter and, if possible, personal presentation of the completed bound transcript by the interviewer and the project director. Some programs have printed up a handsome certificate of participation that can be presented with the transcript or at a later ceremony. From time to time an announcement in the local newspaper can list the recently completed interviews.

Particularly effective is an afternoon reception, perhaps once a year, in the library or a suitable public place, where all the narrators are invited guests of honor and the public is invited to meet them and view the finished transcripts and other memorabilia.

Do not pass up the opportunities to build community identity and to bond the ties between the older and younger generations that are inherent in the public recognition of your narrators.

Curatorship of Oral History Materials

With the deposit of the interview(s) and related materials in an appropriate depository, the processing phase of oral history is completed. But the work is not done. If the interviews are to serve their intended purpose, they must be properly preserved, serviced, publicized, and used.

This passes over into the area of curatorship and involves such considerations as storage conditions for tapes, cataloging, publicity, dissemination of information about holdings to appropriate regional and national information networks, and encouraging users. But that is the subject of another book.

Bibliography

Oral History for the Local Historical Society, by Willa K. Baum. 80 pages, Third Edition, Revised 1987. $9.95 from American Association for State and Local History, 172 Second Avenue North, Suite 202, Nashville, Tennessee 37201. A step-by-step guide to starting an oral history program in your town, selecting the right equipment, and interviewing the people who made history or deserved it.

Oral History—Basic Techniques, edited by Jane McCracken. 20 pages, 1974. $1, from Manitoba Museum, 190 Rupert Avenue, Winnipeg, Manitoba R38 ON2, Canada. Good examples of an interview question outline and an index to an interview.

A Guide for Oral History Programs. 347 pages, 1973. $10, from Oral History Programs, L-330, California State University, Fullerton, California 92634. Includes articles on various aspects of oral history, samples of forms and procedures used at Fullerton, and a catalog of their oral history interviews which indicates how to catalog.

An Oral History Primer, by Gary Shumway and William G. Hartley. 28 pages, 1973. $1.50, from Oral History Program, California State University, Fullerton, address above. A simple guide to how to get going, especially aimed at family history.

A Guide to Aural History Research. $1, from Aural History Program, Provincial Archives of British Columbia, Victoria, British Columbia V8V 1X4, Canada. An excellent manual, especially aimed at making fine sound recordings.

From Tape to Type—An Oral History Manual & Workbook, by Cullom Davis. $4.50, from Oral History Office, Sangamon State University, Springfield, Illinois 62703. An excellent manual.

Oral History As a Teaching Approach, by John A. Neuenschwander. 46 pages, 1976. $2.00, from National Education Association. Order Department, Academic Building, Sawmill Road, West Haven, Connecticut 06516. A brief handbook for the junior high through college social science teacher who wants to use the oral history method as a teaching technique.

Oral History Program Manual, by William W. Moss. 109 pages, 1974. $13.50, from Praeger Publishers, New York, New York. A thoughtful consideration of how to set up a large scale oral history project, based on the experiences of the J. F. Kennedy Oral History Program. This book is essential for the serious, scholarly oral historian planning a substantial program.

The Practice of Oral History, A Handbook, by Ramon I. Harris, Joseph H. Cash, Herbert T. Hoover, and Stephen Ward. 98 pages, 1975. $8.50 from Microfilming Corporation of America, 21 Harristown Road, Glen Rock, New Jersey 07452. Based on the American Indian Oral History Project at the University of South Dakota, this slim handbook has useful guidelines for field work, but at $8.50 is overpriced.

Tape Recorders and Tapes

"The Handling and Storage of Magnetic Recording Tape," in *Sound Talk,* Vol. III, No. 1, 1970. Free, from Product Communications, 3M Company, 3M Center, St. Paul, Minnesota 55101. An excellent basic booklet on how to store tapes.

Recording Basics. $1, from 3M Company, address above.

Care and Handling of Magnetic Recording Tape, 11 pages, 1976. Ampex Corporation, 401 Broadway, Redwood City, California 94063. Free. A simple, straightforward little guide that every oral history program should send for.

LEGAL ASPECTS

"Legal Considerations in Oral History," by Joseph Romney, in *Oral History Review, 1973.* $3, from Oral History Association, P.O. Box 13734, North Texas State University, Denton, Texas 76203. The best summary on legal agreements available.

"Constitutional Liberty and the Law of Libel," by Alfred H. Kelley, in *American Historical Review,* December, 1968. Relationship of libel or slander laws to oral history.

Forms Manual. $8, from Society of American Archivists, P. O. Box 8198, University of Illinois at Chicago Circle, Chicago, Illinois 60680. Examples of legal releases, interview abstracts, application to use tape forms collected from several oral history programs. The manual also includes useful forms that deal with other library functions.

Oral History In General

Oral History Association publications listed below are available from the OHA, P.O. Box 13734, North Texas State University, Denton, Texas 76203. Reduced prices for members.

Oral History in the United States, A Directory, 1971. $1.50, from OHA. A now-outdated but still useful list of oral history projects in the U.S., arranged by state and indexed by subject emphasis.

Bibliography on Oral History, 1975. $3, from OHA. An annotated bibliography of almost everything written about oral history before 1974.

Oral History at Arrowhead, 1966. $3, from OHA. Proceedings from the first conference on oral history.

Selections from the Fifth and Sixth National Colloquia on Oral History, 1970 and 1971. $3, from OHA. Contains useful articles, especially one on how to properly identify an interview on the tape box and transcript and in the library catalog.

Oral History Review, 1973, 1974, 1975. 1973 and 1974, $3 each; 1975, $3.50, from OHA. Selections from the previous year's colloquim, each issue contains significant articles on such subjects as legal considerations, ethics, oral history in teaching, oral history with ethnic groups, oral history in Canada and Great Britain.

"History, Warm," by Louis Starr, 1962. Free, from Oral History Research Office, Box 20, Butler Library, Columbia University, New York, New York 10027.

"Oral History: Problems & Prospects," by Louis M. Starr, in *Advances in Librarianship, Volume II,* edited by Melvin J. Voigt. From Seminar Press, New York, New York, 1971. A comprehensive overview of the field.

Oral History and the Mythmakers, by Charles T. Morrissey. 12 pages, 1964. Preservation Leaflet Series. From National Trust for Historic Preservation, 740–748 Jackson Place, Northwest, Washington, D.C. 20006.

"Oral History: Defining the Term," by Elizabeth Rumics, in *Wilson Library Bulletin 40,* March, 1966. Discusses how oral history differs from recorded sound.

"The Implications of Oral History for Librarians," by Martha Jane Zachert, in *College and Research Libraries* 29, March, 1968. An important article for the librarian handling oral history materials.

Catholic Library World, October, 1975. $2, from Catholic Library Association, 461 West Lancaster Avenue, Haverford, Pennsylvania 19041. This entire issue is devoted to oral history in the library, the association between oral histories and libraries, examples of local history collecting and national history collecting, and examples of how to accession and catalog oral history tapes and transcripts. A must for libraries handling oral history materials.

Sound Heritage, Vol. III, No. 1, 1974. $2, from Aural History Institute of British Columbia, 40 Provincial Archives, Parliament Building, Victoria, British Columbia V8V 1X4, Canada. This issue includes an article on how to use oral history in radio broadcasts.

Oral History, No. 4: The Interview in Social History. £1 (about $2) from Paul Thompson, Department of Sociology, University of Essex, Colchester, CO4 3SQ, England. This issue of *Oral History,* the journal of the British Oral History Society, contains many useful articles on interviewing.

Southern Exposure, Winter, 1974. $2.75, from Institute for Southern Studies, 88 Walton Street, Northwest, Atlanta, Georgia 30303. This issue, entitled *No More Moanin', Voices of Southern Struggle,* includes the best updated bibliography on oral history, emphasis on history-from-the-bottom-up, that has come out since 1971.

CATALOGS OF ORAL HISTORY
Programs

Many programs publish a catalog that can be obtained free or at cost by writing to them. Use *Oral History in the United States, A Directory* as a guide to projects and subjects of emphasis.

The Oral History Collection of Columbia University, edited by Elizabeth B. Mason and Louis M. Starr. 500 pages, 1973. Hardcover $12.50; softcover $7.50, from Oral History Research Office, Box 20, Butler Library, Columbia University, New York, New York 10027. An essential guide for scholars of recent U.S. history, but too large to serve as an example for small oral history projects.

A Guide to the Oral History Program of the Historical Department, the Church of Jesus Christ of Latter-day Saints. 47 pages, 1975. $1.25, from 50 East North Temple, Room 245E, Salt Lake City, Utah 84150. This catalog to the Mormon's oral history program is an excellent example of how to organize a catalog. It includes a description of how their project operates.

JOURNALS AND BOOKS ILLUSTRATING
THE USE OF ORAL HISTORY

Forest History, October, 1972. $2, from Forest History Society, P. O. Box 1581, Santa Cruz, California 95060. Devoted entirely to the Society's oral history program, this issue is a "must" for anyone planning to edit oral history transcripts for journal publication.

Foxfire 1, 2, and 3, edited by Eliot Wigginton. Approximately $5, paperback, from Anchor Press/Doubleday New York, New York. Interviews with old timers of Appalachia, conducted by Rabun Gap, Georgia, high school students. These interviews, edited and published with photographs and drawings by the students, have started a new method in historical teaching.

Akenfield: Portrait of an English Village, by Ronald Blythe. 318 pages, 1969. $2.45, from Dell Publishing Company, New York, New York. A composite of interviews with inhabitants of an English farm village.

By Myself, I'm a Book. An Oral History of the Immigrant Experience in Pittsburgh, prepared by the Pittsburgh Section, National Council of Jewish Women. 166 pages, 1972. $6.50, from American Jewish Historical Society, 2 Thornton Road, Waltham, Massachusetts 02154. An example of an ethnic immigrant project. The arrangement of the book is based on the questionnaire used.

To Be an Indian, an Oral History, edited by Joseph H. Cash and Herbert T. Hoover. 239 pages, 1971. $4, from Holt, Rinehart & Winston, New York, New York. Excerpts from interviews with Indians conducted under the auspices of the Doris Duke Indian History Project.

Plain Speaking: An Oral Biography of Harry S. Truman, by Merle Miller. 480 pages, 1973. $1.95, from Berkley Publishing Corporation, New York, New York. Good example of how to put together excerpts of interviews with the chief narrator and with other narrators.

Hard Times: An Oral History of the Great Depression in America, by Studs Terkel. 462 pages, 1970. $8.95, from Pantheon Books, Random House, New York, New York. An outstanding example of interviewing and selecting excerpts of interviews on a major theme. Terkel's more recent *Working* is the same kind of book.

These Are Our Lives. 421 pages, 1975. Paperback reprint. $4.95, from Norton, New York, New York. Interviews with people of North Carolina, Tennessee and Georgia by members of the Federal Writers Project. Especially useful are the instructions to writers and the outline for life histories.

All God's Dangers: The Life of Nate Shaw, interviewer, Theodore Rosengarten. $2.25, from Avon Books, New York, New York, $12.50, from Alfred Knopf Publishers, New York, New York. Oral history of a black sharecropper. Winner of the 1975 National Book Award.